Front Cover

left
Patsy Gallagher
Charlie Tully
Tommy Gemmell
Kenny Dalglish
Billy McNeill

centre
Paul McStay

right
Jimmy McGrory
Jock Stein
Jimmy Johnstone
Bobby Lennox
Tommy Burns

The Now You Know column in the *Evening Times* is arguably the longest-running sports item in British newspapers.

Fans write in on all manner of sporting topics, not least on matters concerning Glasgow Celtic FC. Over many years columnist and widely respected sports commentator, Bob Crampsey has tried to answer queries and give the facts about the affairs, past and present, of this great club.

NOW YOU KNOW *ABOUT* ... CELTIC is a compilation of the major points of correspondence and a selection of around 200 questions that have occupied the minds of letter-writers.

An invaluable treasure trove of information on the proud traditions of Celtic.

now you know *about* . . .
CELTIC

Bob Crampsey

© Bob Crampsey & *Evening Times* 1994

Published
Argyll Publishing
Glendaruel
Argyll PA22 3AE
in association with
Evening Times
195 Albion Street
Glasgow G1 1QP

British Library Cataloguing-in-Publication Data.
A catalogue record for this book is available from the
British Library.
ISBN 1 874640 16 5

Typeset and origination
Cordfall Ltd, 041 332 4640

Printing
HarperCollins, Glasgow

Contents

Seventy Years and More of Now You Know

The Now You Know column in the *Evening Times* is almost certainly the longest continuous-running sports column in Britain. It has been going since the mid-1920s at least and possibly before that. When I took over the column in 1972 it had been for many years in the hands of the redoubtable Jimmy McCormack (Jaymak) who spared no individual or sporting body in his passion for the correct answer and maintained vehemently that fact and opinion were two completely different things.

To read the answers to past questions is to sit in on the industrial history of a vanished West of Scotland for the questions arising were clearly the subject of discussion at engineering benches, in the Clyde yards and down the pits. The great tradition of the column is that correspondents use *noms de plume* (or aliases) rather than their own names and there was a time when the column was awash with letters from such as Caulker, Riveter's Hauder-On, Yarrow's, Hoover Hand, N. B. Loco, Springburn, and Pit Deputy. All such are now gone as if they had never been. The letters themselves still range in style from notes scribbled on crumpled paper with a blunt pencil to elegantly presented daisy-wheel compositions on headed notepaper.

Celtic and Rangers fans have the very natural human trait in common that they want to read of their many great successes and to skip over their defeats and disasters. That does not mean that the latter go unrecorded for in an Old Firm situation the "other side" will always seek out such information under the guise of a kindly concern for knowledge!

What the questions do is to indicate firmly the players who have established a special place in the hearts and minds of the support. Naturally as the questions come in over the long years some players take a lower profile. But the Quinns, the Gallaghers and the McGrorys survive even although anyone who saw Peerless Patsy play is now well into his 80s. The stars – few in number for it is an over-worked word – the genuine stars, continue to shine even amid all the new developments of competitive European football, the torrent of foreign players and the twin transformers of floodlighting and television. In fact the twins are triplets, sponsorship being the other.

Good times produce more questions than bad. Perhaps the only time when the postbag consistently contained more Celtic than Rangers questions was towards the end of the great Stein era. Predictably the last three or four dismal years have seen a slight falling-off which it would only take one trophy to restore.

Certain topics are hardy annuals, almost hardy monthlies. Did A ever play in the same side as B? The answer to this one is almost always yes, although there may be as much as 15 years between the ages of the two players. "The chap on the next bench to me says he was on Celtic's books in 1935. Is this true?" The answer to this one is almost always no, the statement being an incautious boast late on in a pub. Just occasionally white man does not speak with forked tongue and can be justified in the column to his own great delight and the combined annoyance and veneration of his workmates.

We are not the innovators that we sometimes like to think we are and few things are new under the sun. There was floodlit football of a sort a century and more ago and Celtic had foreign and coloured players a full sixty years before popular opinion might credit it.

A word of caution here. My own commitment is, as it has to be in the column, to Scottish football in general and this inevitably means that in every senior club and most junior ones there are a few people whose knowledge of their own single club is greater than mine. This does not matter greatly for when mistakes occur I have been touched and humbled by the almost invariable courtesy with which my correspondents draw attention to my errors or omissions.

What then are the desires of the Celtic fans? Above all else, to be a force in Europe again. The years between 1967-72 gave them a taste for high living which they have never lost. In the recent turmoils several things have emerged, some of which I dealt with on radio and television mindful of my great predecessor's dictum that the column deals in facts! It is clear however that Celtic fans wish to stay at Parkhead, that they hope to have a good stadium but realistically do not believe one can be built as good as the new Ibrox, and in any case they see the absolute priority as the team on the field.

They want to get back to winning cups again and they want to feel that with regard to the managership things are settled and tranquil for a while. They would like to see some stability in the playing staff. They are right to want this for a great part of supporting a club is the establishing of a long-term relationship between player and fans.

The support have welcomed the recent arrival of Fergus McCann and his new broom. They wish him well and are very anxious that their own importance to the club should be recognised and first signs are that this will be so. He would appear to combine the necessary business acumen with the feeling for the club which is so vital.

Where this happens something quite wonderful takes place. Players such as Delaney, John Thomson, McGrory and more recently McNeill and Dalglish live on vividly in the memories of those who at best last saw them play 20 years ago or even stranger, never saw them play at all.

No one can understand the industrial West of Scotland fully who does not understand association football and in particular the weird inter-dependence of the Old Firm. The story of the last century has largely been one of Rangers domination in the League interspersed with remarkable surges by Celtic which saw them take the title four, six and finally nine times in succession. In the Scottish Cup, Celtic have always had the edge as they had in reaching consecutive League Cup finals, though not in winning once they had got there.

I hope very much that the answers to the questions in this book will inform and entertain and I have interspersed them with various short essays on the topics to try to place them in perspective. Remember that naturally most of the questions deal with time past. Most people recall the details of last week's match, at least in the short term. Inevitably some of the answers which were correct at the time of being written have been overtaken by subsequent events. Wherever possible I have tried to give the date at which the answer was originally given but this is the only form of editing that has taken place.

For those old enough to remember, I hope the memories return of the No 9 Auchenshuggle car wobbling out London Road on the way to the early winter kick-offs of those pre-floodlit times. Of the cries of the optimistic sellers of food, "Fourpence ra meat and cheese sandwidges". Of the tireless vendor and his "Erzi offishal program". Of the twinkling pinpoints of light as the crowd, smokers to a man, lit and constantly re-lit Woodbines, Prize Crop or Capstan Full Strength. Of the days when the reserve side was the Alliance side and players wore heavy woollen jerseys with lace-up collars and the lace-up boots that, in the famous words of Hugh McIlvanney, "chafed you under the armpits." When the T panel ball became as heavy as lead on a muddy day, needing not only skill but courage to head it and when in a downpour the same heavy woollen jerseys came to weigh a ton.

A last word of introduction. I am not at all a fan of those videos where the opposing team never gets over the halfway line let alone scores a goal. I have therefore included a modest proportion of answers on matches where victory did not on that day crown the brow. Any account of total unrelieved success is not only boring but inaccurate. The greatest triumphs are best savoured after previous adversity.

It was precisely this that has elevated Jock Stein to unchallenged supremacy in the temple of the Parkhead gods. There will therefore be no sentences in this book along the lines of, "In the final we were unlucky to be beaten 7-1." Or even 8-1!

CHAPTER ONE

Celtic in Europe

There is no doubt that Europe has been Celtic's crowning glory, especially the five years between 1965-70 when they played a leading role not just in Scottish or even British football but in the Continental game as well. During this period accounts of their exploits filled not only the British press but such publications as the French *L'Equipe* and the Spanish *Marca*.

It was a scene entered on with faltering steps and one on which other Scottish clubs like Hibernian, Hearts and Rangers had already trod. To be a player in the European league it was necessary to win things and Celtic were perhaps a shade unlucky that their 1957 League Cup win over Rangers did not bring the automatic entry to European competition that it would have done a few years later.

So it was that their first European involvement had a nice touch of farce about it. Celtic were invited to play in a most undistinguished Franco-Scottish tournament known as the Friendship Cup in which they lost in the first round to a club of no great account, Sedan. It hardly mattered as things turned out, for the competition had no discernible shape and collapsed unfinished in a flurry of acrimony.

It would be 1962-63 before the club had its first taste of pukka European football and straight away they were pitched into a Fairs Cities Cup (later the UEFA Cup) against the holders Valencia. They did not survive this experience losing 4-2 in Spain and drawing 2-2 back home. The tie afforded two interesting questions for future reference. These were, "Who scored Celtic's first goal in European competition proper?" – the unlikely answer being Mestre of Barcelona, own goal. And, "Who missed Celtic's first-ever penalty in Europe?" – the almost equally unlikely answer being John Clark.

Gradually Celtic were getting the temperature of the bath water and it seemed great things might be done in 1963-64 when in the Cup Winners Cup, even although entry had been by the back door, a highly respectable list of opponents, namely Basle, Dinamo Zagreb and Slovan Bratislava, were despatched. When MTK Budapest departed Parkhead on the wrong end of a 3-0 scoreline it seemed a final place was the worst Celtic could do.

Only 10,000 Hungarians thought it worth while turning up for the return – five times as many had watched at Parkhead – but the Hungarians got the early goal. Celtic had two knocked off for offside, correctly was the general verdict, the defence panicked and over the two games 3-0 became 3-4. Europe would not yield its secrets quite so easily.

So to Jimmy McGrory's last season in charge in Europe and the question, "In which match in Europe was more than one Celtic player sent off for the first time?" Portugal the location, Leixoes the opposition, Ian Young and the mild-mannered Steve Chalmers the men expelled. Celtic still got a 1-1 draw and bundled the Portuguese over comfortably at home. A bad draw which saw them face the mighty Barcelona seemed to promise disaster when the Spaniards scored two early goals in Spain and Clark had to cripple on the wing for 55 minutes in those pre-substitute days. A John Hughes goal early in the second-half offered some hope but Barcelona got a third goal and a blank sheet at Parkhead looking round them.

"Against which major footballing nation have Celtic scored six goals away from home?" Answer Holland, Go Ahead Deventer absolutely going astern on the night in question. The return was a formality, the only noteworthy thing about it being the fact that 20,000 thought it worth coming out to a match which their

A rustic setting for a European final – Bobby Murdoch just fails to connect with a cross at Lisbon in May 1967

favourites started six goals ahead. In quick succession the Danish team Aarhus and the Russians Dynamo Kiev were defeated and by the time Liverpool were encountered in the semi-final Jock Stein had arrived. There were 80,000 to see the first leg at Parkhead and great rejoicing when Bobby Lennox scored the only goal. The more battle-weary supporters were of the opinion that if Celtic could not defend three goals in Budapest they would certainly not defend one in Liverpool.

The cynics had it. A Celtic team lacking Johnstone defended stoutly but the game plan was upset by two Liverpool goals in five minutes on the hour mark, and although a switch to attack was made and a Lennox goal disallowed on a marginal decision, Liverpool went through to the final which perversely was due to be played at Hampden that year.

And so to 1967, the Wonder Year. Zurich and Nantes caused no problems, and of course for the first time we are talking of the major trophy, the European Cup. A match with a Yugoslav side, hard and skilful as they were, was always to be avoided by choice but Celtic and Vojvodina were paired. Things were going well for Celtic who were slowly learning how to defend when suddenly the marvellously flamboyant Tommy Gemmell was short with a pass-back and hopelessly stranded John Clark and Ronnie Simpson.

A curious error surrounds the return at Parkhead. Many letters arrive which clearly imagine that Billy McNeill's injury-time header from a Charlie Gallagher corner prevented Celtic from losing the game. Not so. Neither side had scored away and the outcome of McNeill not scoring would have been a play-off at Rotterdam. It was not needed and in the semi-final Dukla Prague retired from the field at Parkhead 3-1 down. Not bad but would it be enough? By virtue of playing what Robert Kelly called the "most defensive performance he had ever seen from a Celtic side in his life", a 0-0 draw was got without too much stress.

So to the final and a collection of letters based on myth. Did Celtic supporters end up in Italy on the wrong plane? How many supporters never came home at all? And the one unanswerable, how many were in the welcoming crowd back home in Glasgow? Question, "Who was the Rangers' chairman who was in the crowd?" Answer, John Lawrence and he deserves to be remembered for a brave and generous action.

Did Celtic have a substitute that day? Yes, John Fallon was the designated reserve goalkeeper. Did Ronnie Simpson really back-heel the ball in a European Cup Final? Answer, he did. Did Bill Shankly say to Jock Stein, "Jock, you're immortal."? No, he said, "John, you're immortal." Close friends and people who had known him all his life tended to call him John.

The Argentina and Uruguay fiascos with Racing Club are really nothing to do with the European section although the Montevideo game – with three sent off from the Celtic side and Bertie Auld electing not to go – calls into question the continuance of the match if he had removed himself and Celtic had then been left with only seven men afield.

Not surprisingly there was a reaction the following year with old opponents Dynamo Kiev winning 2-1 at Parkhead, against the Lisbon Lions at that, and then scoring in Russia in the very last minute to go through on a 1-1 draw. This was heart-breaking as Bobby Murdoch had taken the long walk after 59 minutes for throwing the ball away, a very avertible and extremely costly sending-off.

Things were better in 1968-69 although it looked like being a short campaign when St Etienne in the last-minute of the first-half at Parkhead retained the two-goal lead they had established in France. Then came a real home-town penalty which Tommy Gemmell thundered home and in the second half a justifiably aggrieved French side conceded three more goals.

There followed one of the great performances in the club's history as Jimmy Johnstone, promised that he need not go to Belgrade if the match was effectively decided at Parkhead, tore the Red Star defence apart in an astounding display of virtuosity at speed. Stein the canny man ever, tried to get Johnstone to go anyway but the little flame-haired winger was emphatic that a deal was a deal. What wonders we might have seen had Stein told

Johnstone that from now on Celtic intended to fly to all away matches in Scotland!

In the semi-final in Milan, where huskies and snowshoes would have been more appropriate, Celtic got a creditable if very dull 0-0 draw. That is a dangerous score in Europe though because, should the opposition score second time round, then the home side needs to register twice. The Italians got their goal after only twelve minutes at Parkhead, McNeill and Craig being momentarily on different wavelengths and AC Milan demonstrated yet again that in the art of defending a single goal lead away from home, the Italians have no superiors.

The year 1970 marks the high-water mark of Celtic's time in Europe. Out went Basle, out went Benfica, but only on the toss of a coin after a 3-0 home lead had been squandered. Fiorentina were comfortably vanquished and then to great national joy Leeds United were overcome home and away. Question, "Did Celtic ever wear orange socks in a European Cup tie?" Answer, Yes – in the first of the matches against Leeds United at Elland Road .

Leeds having been eliminated, surely the scarcely-regarded Feyenoord would pose no obstacle to a second European success? Alas! this was the classic case of skinning the bear before it was caught. Stein himself admitted that his approach to the match had been over-casual and perhaps because of this the supporters had noticed that the team on the night played as though at odds with itself.

And since then, final triumph has never been so near. In 1970-71, 14 goals against the Finnish strugglers Kokkola and 10 against Waterford were no preparation for Ajax, who were becoming the European force that Celtic had been. Certainly a three goal deficit incurred in Holland was not recoverable at Hampden. There was a false dawn a year later when the ball lay on the spot at Parkhead at the beginning of a penalty shoot-out with Inter Milan who had played two 0-0 draws of numbing boredom. Dixie Deans blazed the ball fiercely over the bar and Inter went on to avenge 1967.

Italians are better than Scots at playing the cold, intelligent

It's there! Steve Chalmers gets the deflection to a Bobby Murdoch shot which gave Celtic the European Cup in May 1967

defensive long-haul and when Celtic tried that method of defending a one-goal lead against Ujpest Dosza in 1973 they were quite unable to move to Plan B on finding themselves three down after 22 minutes. By now they had slipped from top European ranking and needed extra time to beat such run of the mill opponents as the Swiss side Basle. They might also have wished that they had not as in the quarter-final they were subjected to incessant thuggery from the Spanish side Atletico Madrid. Question, "How many Atletico players were sent off? Answer, three. Question, "Why did not Celtic make this enormous numerical advantage tell?" A matter of opinion.

When did Celtic first wear numbers on their backs? Against Boavista in November 1975. This was a good win but the mediocre Sachsenring Zwickau from East Germany eliminated Celtic at the quarter-final stage and Stein knew what many had long suspected, the game for the moment was up.

The following year their conquerors were Wisla Krakow of Poland, scarcely a household word but capable of avoiding defeat even at Parkhead. Interest tended to switch to the fringe players introduced against the minnows in the early round so that the 6'4" McWilliams from Queen's Park and John McCluskey, younger brother of George made very rare first-team appearances in the European Cup. Indeed McCluskey has a European Cup match as his only first-team outing.

Jock Stein's marvellous reign in Europe ended with a whimper, a 3-0 defeat from the indifferent SWW Innsbruck and the sending-off of Andy Lynch. As playing standards deteriorated, so too did on-field discipline.

How far the club had sunk was demonstrated vividly in 1978-79 when for the first time in almost 18 years there was no European football at all. In its place came the cobbled-up Anglo-Scottish Cup and an embarrassing defeat at the hands of Burnley long since departed the top flight of English sides. Question, "Had the two sides ever met in a cup-tie before?" Answer, Yes, in their capacity as English and Scottish Cup winners in 1914 when a trophy was put up for a challenge match.

There were still good one-off performances. To beat Real Madrid at home, even in 1980 was a notable feat. But once again the team could not perform away from home. The Rumanian side Politechnica Timisoara got through after giving themselves a life line with a late goal at Parkhead which made 2-0 into 2-1. The following year Juventus lost at Parkhead but by now Celtic were as soft as putty in the away legs. Which manager of the club destroyed Celtic in a European Cup-tie? Answer, Liam Brady who orchestrated a 2-0 win for Juventus.

Celtic were not a million miles from success and in 1982-83 they reversed a trend by securing a dangerous draw against Ajax at home but then winning the return in Holland. The following year they seemed to have done most of the job with a very good draw against Nottingham Forest at the City Ground. But this result became almost inexplicable when Forest revealed a vast difference in class in beating Celtic 2-1.

The taste for Europe was almost lost totally when Rapid Vienna, having been eliminated 4-3 on aggregate, managed to persuade UEFA to order a re-run at Old Trafford. Once more all-out attack left the door unguarded and the composed Austrians took full advantage. This had ramifications for the following year when Celtic were condemned to play their next home match in Europe behind closed doors. They did well to hold Atletico Madrid to a 1-1 draw in Spain, courtesy of a superb Maurice Johnston goal, but in the eerie, empty Parkhead which greeted the return match, the methodical Spaniards went two ahead before Roy Aitken pulled a meaningless goal back.

And so it went on – progress in Europe absolutely depending on drawing a minnow early on. So what went wrong? Firstly, a really good European side rarely stays at the top for more than five years and Celtic certainly managed that. Secondly, an increasing pattern developed of good players, and especially forwards being transferred. The 70s and 80s were a story of the departure of such as Dalglish, Macari, Nicholas and McClair.

Yet what cannot be gainsaid is that Celtic in the 1960s put Scottish football in the forefront of Europe. It gave other Scots clubs the knowledge that success could be had at this level and Celtic's win was to be followed by others for Rangers and Aberdeen.

The memories? The calm and composed way Celtic worked to prise open the seemingly watertight Inter Milan defence in 1967, and Jimmy Johnstone's *tour de force* against Red Star perhaps the greatest ever display by a Celtic player. The header by Billy McNeill against Vojvodina, provided by the unsung and under-estimated Charlie Gallagher. The times when the Continentals, under severe pressure, stole away on the break with the speed of a cobra to score a goal in stricken silence.

But more important was the feeling that these were important games, that they mattered, that the club was at the heart of things. All things in football are cyclical and it is as certain as makes no difference that when the stadium is eventually rebuilt and re-opened, the best of Europe will again be queuing up to try conclusions with a Celtic side which it may be hoped will have regained its composure, its skill and its sense of tradition.

CELTIC IN EUROPE

TOM JAY Can you give the time of the kick-off and when the TV transmission started in the Celtic v Inter Milan final of 1967?
The kick-off was at 5.30 p.m. and the BBC started the transmission of the whole match ten minutes earlier.

MARINE BLUENOSE (Singapore) To settle a dispute I have had with a Celtic fan in our group can you confirm that in season 1963-64 in either the European Cup or the Fairs Cities Cup Celtic won 3-0 against MTK at Parkhead and were beaten 4-0 in the away game.
This happened on April 15 and April 29, 1964 in the semi-final of the Cup Winners Cup (note competition).

THE BOLT, HASTIE'S (Greenock) Who was the Celtic player ordered off in Russia against Dynamo Kiev? Was it Jim Craig or Bobby Murdoch?

Bobby Murdoch was sent off after 57 minutes of this European Cup second leg in 1967-68. The result was a 1-1 draw.

JOLLY GREEN GIANT (Glasgow) Are Celtic the only team to appear in the European Cup in eight successive years up till now (1973)? Did they beat Penarol when the latter were World Champions? Has any other side won everything played for as Celtic did in 1967?

Celtic's record of eight successive appearances until 1973 is comfortably surpassed by Real Madrid. Penarol were World Champions when beaten by Celtic in September 1967. Rangers won everything they competed for in season 1929-30 and I fancy Linfield have also done this in Northern Ireland.

TOP LEFT (Dumbarton) In the Cup Winners Cup of 1963 or 1964 Celtic beat Slovan Bratislava 1-0 at Parkhead through a Bobby Murdoch penalty kick. Did John Hughes miss a penalty in the same match?

Reports give the score and scorer as you say, the date being February 26, 1964 but make no reference to a missed penalty.

T. LOVE (Glasgow) I claim that Celtic have beaten five clubs, Penarol, Racing Club, Real Madrid, Ajax and AC Milan who have held the title of World Champions.

You are correct in so far as Celtic have beaten all these teams over ninety minutes. Some might argue that the Racing and Ajax matches were to be decided over two legs but certainly Celtic have recorded victories over all five clubs.

TAXIS (Glasgow) Did Celtic beat Fiorentina in the European Cup in 1970 or 1971?

It was in the spring of 1970 that Celtic beat the Italian club, winning 3-0 at home and losing 1-0 away before going down to Feyenoord in the final.

DANNY McDERMOTT (Hamilton) In addition to the winning team at Lisbon what other Celtic players took part in the European Cup triumph that year?

Four other players took part at various stages that year and they were Willie O'Neill, John Hughes, Joe McBride and Charlie Gallagher.

BOSTON BEAN (Dennistoun) Give the score, scorers, crowd and nationality of the referee when Liverpool beat Celtic in the Cup Winners Cup at Anfield in 1966.

The match was played on April 19, Liverpool winning 2-0 through goals by Smith and Strong. The crowd was 52,000 and the referee M J Hamnet was from Belgium.

TINY TIM (Barrowfield) What was the Celtic side (including substitutes) in the 1970 European Cup Final against Feyenoord. Please give score and scorers.

Celtic lost this match 2-1 with the following side, Williams, Hay, Gemmell, Murdoch, McNeill, Brogan, Johnstone, Lennox, Wallace, Auld, Hughes. In the second half Connelly came on for Auld. Gemmell scored for Celtic and Van Dyk and Haan for Feyenoord.

TIM (Glasgow) When Billy McNeill scored the winner against Vojvodina, was the corner taken from the ground side or the stand side?

As I remember the incident the corner was taken from the stand side by Charlie Gallagher.

CALLING D.C. (Glasgow)

You are quite right in thinking that two Celtic players have been sent off against Dynamo Kiev. When I mentioned Bobby Murdoch in season 1967-68 I had temporarily forgotten that Jim Craig also took the walk in the Cup Winners tournament in 1965-66.

BILL (Cambuslang) Please give goal times in the Celtic v St Etienne match at Parkhead when Celtic were two down from the first leg.

Celtic won this return 4-0 in the 1968-69 European Cup. Their scorers were Gemmell (pen.45), Craig (59), Chalmers (67) and McBride (87).

R.H.OTIS (Glasgow) Which Scottish team was the first to beat Celtic after their European Cup win?

Opposite
Jimmy Johnstone leaves the field after his great virtuoso performance against Red Star at Parkhead – a fan shakes his head in wonderment

After Celtic won in Lisbon they were undefeated in competitive matches in Scotland until Rangers beat them 1-0 at Ibrox on September 16, 1967.

JOHN COGAN (Wishaw) Did Kenny Dalglish play for Celtic in the European Cup tie in which Dixie Deans shot over the bar from the penalty spot?

Dalglish did play in this match and ironically he was substituted by Deans.

COWBOY (Clydebank) In which season was the Celtic-Atletico Madrid match in which two Spaniards were ordered off?

This match , a goalless draw was played in 1974 and note that the Turkish referee, Dogan Barbacan, sent off three Atletico players.

MICHAEL UPSTART (Coatbridge) When Celtic played Dukla Prague in the European Cup semi-final of 1967 was either of the two matches televised live?

No. The Parkhead match had highlights shown at 11 p.m. and the return in Prague had highlights shown at 6.15 p.m. but the kick-off in Czechoslovakia had been at 4 p.m.

JAMIE (Victoria Bar) After Celtic had beaten Red Star 5-1 in a European Cup match did Jimmy Johnstone travel to Yugoslavia for the second leg?

No. He had been promised exemption because of his dislike of flying if he helped Celtic to achieve a satisfactory result in the first leg. He was not listed in the side which drew 1-1 in Belgrade in season 1968-69.

CALVAY (Barlanark) What were Celtic's results in European competitions in seasons 1979-80 and 1980-81?

In 1979-80 in the European Cup Celtic lost 1-0 away to Partisan Tirana but won the return 4-1. They then beat Dundalk 3-2 at home and drew the return 0-0. In the quarter finals they beat Real Madrid 2-0 at Parkhead but lost 3-0 at Bernabeu. The following year in the Cup Winners they beat Diasgyor 6-0 at home and lost the return 2-1. They then beat Poli Timasoara 2-1 at Parkhead and lost the return 1-0.

CHAPTER TWO

The Scottish Cup

In the popular esteem Celtic are above all else a Scottish Cup side and that competition has provided many of the club's most heart-stopping moments. The newly-born Celtic were quickly into their stride. They could have won the competition in their first year of existence but lost out narrowly to Third Lanark. They were soon to rectify that with a win over Queen's Park in 1892 – nothing could more vividly have illustrated the way that power was shifting in Scottish football.

At this great distance in time, what questions get asked about these early years? One is, who apart from Jimmy Quinn has scored a hat-trick in a Scottish Cup Final? Answer, only another Celtic player, Dixie Deans who scored three against Hibernian in 1972 as Quinn had done against Rangers in 1904. Another is, how many Celtic managers have scored in the Scottish Cup Final. This time the answer is three, Jimmy McGrory, Billy McNeill and Lou Macari and all scored more than once. Still another, why if the Hampden riot was so serious was there only one arrest. Answer, quite simply because it was so serious that the police on duty were instructed not to make any arrests.

Between 1923-27 Celtic won the Scottish Cup three times with three different goalkeepers and the last occasion would see the first of John Thomson's two successes. The tradition of last-minute wins or saves could be said to go back to the final of 1931 against Motherwell when Celtic, resigned almost to defeat, swung a desultory ball into the goalmouth where centre-half Craig, hearing a shout of "Yours, Alan" rose to head into his own net a ball meant for the other Alan, goalkeeper McClory.

The 1937 final against Aberdeen still commands attention because of the crowd size. People never tire of wanting to be told that really, there were more than 146,000 there and fans dwell on the fact that it was an outstandingly good side, which it was – although in fact the extant film of the final shows that the match itself was a pretty dire affair.Even then the successes were made sweeter by the failures. There were depressing home defeats in the Cup in the late 1930s from St Johnstone and Kilmarnock, the latter distinguished by the petulant refusal of the then Celtic manager, Willie Maley, to congratulate a future one, Jimmy McGrory, then in charge of the Ayrshire team. Can you confirm that this happened Bob? It happened.

After the war Celtic took some time to get into their pre-war Cup vein and there was a defeat from Second Division Dundee United which was as damaging as any in the club's history until the recent one from Falkirk in 1993. Things seemed to be getting better when a clever John McPhail chip brought victory in 1951 against Motherwell and when Aberdeen were seen off in the double year of 1954. But the following two finals against Clyde and Hearts were thrown away by a combination of goalkeeping error and weird team selection. Did Celtic really drop Bobby Collins for a Cup final replay? Yes. Did they really play Mike Haughney out of position and up front in the 1956 final against Hearts? Yes.

There followed the wilderness years in which Dunfermline beat a much more fancied Celtic in 1961 and Rangers destroyed them in 1963 until finally Billy McNeill's header did in the Fifers in 1965 and seemed to promise a new era. There was a stumble

Opposite
Bobby Lennox in full flight against Clydebank in the Scottish Cup tie of 1974 which was Celtic's first ever match on a Sunday

Jock Stein and his wife share the Scottish Cup of 1954 with (left) Charlie Tully and (right) Alec Dowdells

the following year when on-form Celtic, not Rangers, should have taken the 1966 Scottish Cup. Question, was Kaj Johansen the first Dane ever to score against Celtic? Answer, no, it had been done more than forty years ago by Carl Hansen.

Then came the great days, the defeat of Aberdeen in 1967, the 4-0 demolition of Rangers in 1969 that at long last brought revenge for the similar margin of defeat in 1928. Rangers went down again in 1971 (name the Celtic player who scored two own goals against Rangers in Scottish Cup ties. Answer, Jim Craig) and in 1972 Celtic ran riot against what was a very good Hibernian side.

Rangers marked their centenary with a 3-2 win in the 1973 final. Question – surely asked with tongue in cheek – how far out was Tom Forsyth when he scored the winner? Preferred answers run from six inches to three feet. But normally around this time if Celtic reached the final they could finish the job and by 1980 in addition to another two final wins over Rangers they had seen off Airdrieonians and Dundee United.

The end of the 1980 final, won by a George McCluskey deflection, was marked by a full-scale riot and trouble seemed closely allied to Scottish Cup finals at this time. In 1984 in an eerie dress rehearsal for 1990 Celtic lost in extra time to Aberdeen and Roy Aitken was sent from the field.

Question, was Roy Aitken the first player to be ordered off in a Scottish Cup final? No, Jock Buchanan of Rangers had blazed the trail for him in 1929.

Since then the final has eluded Celtic but of course the Scottish Cup is not simply about finals. It is possible that some of those who write in wanting details of the two heavy semi-final defeats by St Mirren in 1959 and 1962 are Celtic supporters, sucking as it were on the bad tooth but more probably they are St Mirren fans seeking revenge for the five goals that Neil Mochan scored against them in the Cup in 1960.

There are questions about the cup tie against Clydebank which was Celtic's first Sunday game, about the match in which Elgin City were 1-0 ahead with ten minutes to go, about the last-minute penalty missed by Stranraer which would have taken the tie back to a potentially very dangerous Stair Park. There was the Old Firm tie in 1957 when Celtic blew a 4-2 lead with 15 minutes to go to draw 4-4 but retrieved things with a 2-0 win at Ibrox. There was the injury sustained in a cup tie at Shawfield which eventually wrote finish to Ronnie Simpson's great career and there was not one but two occasions in which Third Lanark and Celtic, having been thwarted by snow in their attempts to play a Scottish Cup tie, rashly offered a friendly match instead, with predictable results on the disorder front.

Scottish Cup ties, especially away from home, fulfilled a most important missionary function and because of this small sedate Scottish towns such as Leith, Lochgelly, Brechin and Dalbeattie were able to see the greats of the inter-war period, with one of the very earliest football films in Scotland being of a visit to Lochgelly by Celtic in the early 1920s. It enables us to get a glimpse on film of such as Patsy Gallagher and Tommy McInally but only a glimpse for the film was made by the owners of the local cinema and was therefore far more concerned with getting the faces of the locals on the screen for the following Saturday night.

For those in search of the quirky, Celtic's last six Scottish Cup successes have involved three different goalkeepers, none of whom was Scottish. The knowlegeable will already have marked them as Peter Latchford, Alan McKnight and Pat Bonner.

Out of all the indelible memories of Celtic in the Scottish Cup perhaps the sharpest is the recovery against Dundee United in 1985 when looking destined for defeat, they were revived by a Davie Provan equaliser from a free kick. Then with no thought of extra time, even so late in the game, they went flat-out for the winner which Frank McGarvey provided.

Opposite
Stateside – John McPhail holds up the Scottish Cup before the start of the tour match of 1951 against the All Star Americans which Celtic won 5-1

What was the connection between that final and the one of 1925? Simple, really. In both finals two brothers called McStay played in the Celtic side against a team from Dundee. Only connect, as my correspondents tell me!

THE SCOTTISH CUP

EXTRA FINAL (Paisley) Which club knocked St Mirren out of the Scottish Cup when they were holders in 1959? Please give teams and scorers.

They were beaten 5-2 after two drawn ties of 1-1 and 4-4. Third game teams at Parkhead were, CELTIC, Haffey, McKay, Kennedy, McNeill, Evans, Peacock, Smith, Colrain, Mochan, Divers, Byrne.

ST MIRREN, Walker, Wilson, Riddell, Neilson, Tierney, McGugan, Rodger, Bryceland, Baker, Gemmell, Miller.

For Celtic Neil Mochan had all five goals with Gemmell and Rodger on the mark for Saints.

THE BELLS BAR (Bridgeton) Teams please in the Celtic v Airdrie Scottish Cup semi-final of 1955.

These matches were played at Hampden and the teams were, AIRDRIE, Walker, Shanks, Gordon, Quinn, Baillie, Cairns, Reid, Welsh, Baird, McMillan, McCulloch.

CELTIC, Bonner, Haughney, Meechan, Evans, Stein, Peacock, Collins, Fernie, Walsh, Mochan, Tully.

In the second game Airdrie were unchanged but Celtic played McPhail at centre-forward and Walsh at inside-left.

DOONHAMER (Dalbeattie) As we are not sure if Jimmy McGrory took part, what were the teams when Dalbeattie Star met Celtic in a Scottish Cup tie around 1934?

Opposite
A joke? Did I remember to take my teeth out? Steve Chalmers seems amused at the antics of Billy McNeill as he leads out the Celtic team for a 1967 cup tie

In the first round at Dalbeattie on January 20, 1934 Celtic won 6-0 and the teams were, DALBEATTIE STAR, Reid, Tyson, Chandler, Ritchie, McLeod, Ancell, Nisbet, Kirkland, Martin, Nicholson, Thomson.

CELTIC, Kennaway, Hogg, McGonagle, Dawson, McStay, Hughes, Napier, Thomson, Crum, O'Donnell, McDonald.

ARGUMENT (Shieldmuir) Was the Celtic v Motherwell Cup Final of 1951 televised?

No, television did not come to Scotland until March 14, 1952. It seems most unlikely that the game would have been transmitted to an English audience only.

CURIOUS (Glasgow) Is it true that Bob McPhail and Jimmy McMenemy each have six Scottish Cup badges?

In fact each has seven, Jimmy McMenemy having won a medal with Partick Thistle and Bob McPhail with Airdrieonians.

DARROCH BAR (Gourock) Can you verify that when Celtic lost to St Mirren in the semi-final of the Scottish Cup in 1959 that they beat St Mirren at Love Street on the Monday of that week?

In 1959 St Mirren beat Celtic 4-0 in the semi-final and three weeks before Celtic had also lost 1-0 at Paisley. I feel you confuse the cup campaign of 1959 with that of 1962.

THE NOGGIN (Uddingston) Please give the winning team and scorers in the 1937 Cup Final. Was the attendance a British record?

Celtic beat Aberdeen 2-1, Crum and Buchan scoring for them, Armstrong for Aberdeen. The victorious Celtic side read, Kennaway, Hogg, Morrison, Geatons, Lyon, Paterson, Delaney, Buchan, McGrory, Crum, Murphy. The attendance of 146, 563 was a record for a British club match.

LONDON ROAD (Glasgow) My pal says that a non-league side once scored three goals against Celtic in a Scottish Cup tie. Is this right?

Quite right. Burntisland Shipyard scored three against Celtic in the first round in 1939 but Celtic replied with eight goals!

FRANCIS MORAN (Easterhouse) Please give the Celtic side

*Celtic manager wins Scottish Cup against them – Jock Stein in Dunfermline's
moment of victory in 1961*

in the Scottish Cup Final of 1965. Also give the scorers.

Celtic won this match 3-2 and here is the team.

CELTIC, Fallon, Young, Gemmell, Murdoch, McNeill, Clark, Chalmers, Gallagher, Hughes, Lennox, Auld. Scorers were Auld (2) and McNeill for Celtic, Melrose and McLaughlin for Dunfermline.

F. M. AGAIN (Easterhouse) When did Bobby Murdoch play his first game at right-half? Was it before the arrival of Jock Stein?

I make him to have filled the right-half spot in a Scottish Cup quarter-final against Rangers in 1964 when Rangers won 2-0 and this would be some time before the arrival of Jock Stein as manager.

TERRY (Glasgow) Has either member of the Old Firm won in a Scottish Cup tie by five clear goals?

Celtic managed this when they beat Rangers 5-0 in the Scottish Cup semi-final of 1925.

JUNGLE JERRY (Carntyne) Confirm that Jock Stein won a Scottish Cup medal against Celtic?

He did this in 1961 while managing Dunfermline Athletic when the Fifers won a replay 2-0 after a goalless draw on the Saturday.

SILVER SANDS (Saltcoats) Please give the sides that played in the first match of the 1931 Scottish Cup Final. Were two of the Celtic players dead inside two years?

Teams in the 2-2 draw were, CELTIC, J Thomson, Cook, McGonagle, Wilson, McStay, Geatons, R Thomson, A Thomson, McGrory, Scarff, Napier.

MOTHERWELL, McClory, Johnman, Hunter, Wales, Craig, Telfer, Murdoch, McMenemy, McFadyen, Stevenson, Ferrier. Of that Celtic side John Thomson was killed the following September and Peter Scarff died of tuberculosis in December 1933.

WINDSOR (Bargeddie) Is it true that Willie Fernie was twice in consecutive losing Scottish Finals?

Yes, against Clyde in 1955 and Hearts in 1956 and then against

Dunfermline Athletic in 1961 and (with St Mirren) against Rangers in 1962.

TRUE TIM (Glasgow) Can you confirm that to date (1976) Rangers have not beaten Celtic in a Scottish Cup tie at Parkhead for 71 years?

Celtic last lost to Rangers in a semi-final at Parkhead in 1905 when the Ibrox men won 2-0.

BIG TAM (Glasgow) Have Celtic ever lost to a non-league side in the Scottish Cup?

You have to go back to 1897 for this when they lost 4-2 to Arthurlie at Barrhead.

TED (Falkirk) Please give scorers and crowd in the replay of the Scottish Cup Final of 1931.

Celtic took the Cup beating Motherwell 4-2 after a 2-2 draw. Celtic scorers were McGrory (2) and R Thomson (2) with Murdoch and Stevenson scoring for Motherwell before 99,000 spectators.

050 (Glasgow East) Can you trace a Celtic player who played in five consecutive Scottish Cup Finals?

I have an answer which almost fits the bill in that McAteer played in five consecutive matches. These were three for Clyde against Dundee in the 1910 final and then two for Celtic against Hamilton Academicals the following year.

CONCORD BAR (Tollcross) Did Celtic as Scottish Cup winners play Cardiff City as English Cup winners at Celtic Park in the late 1920s? If so please give teams and scorers.

On October 3, 1927 Celtic beat Cardiff City 4-1 at Parkhead. CELTIC, J Thomson, W McStay, McGonagle, Wilson, J McStay, McFarlane, A Thomson, McMenemy, McGrory, McInally, Connelly.

CARDIFF CITY, Farquharson, Nelson, Hardy, Irving, Keenor, Pirie, Thirlaway, Davies, Ferguson, Curtis, Cook.

All Celtic's goals fell to McGrory with Curtis scoring for Cardiff City.

AIRBLES CROWN (Motherwell) How many medals did Paddy Connelly win in the Scottish Cup with Celtic?

He was in three winning sides, against Hibernian in 1923, Dundee in 1925 and East Fife in 1927. He also appeared in the losing finals of 1926 and 1928 against St Mirren and Rangers.

PAT AND CHAS (Clydebank) Did George Best ever play in a Scottish Cup tie against Celtic?

He wore the No 11 jersey for Hibernian on April 12, 1980 when his side lost 5-0 at Hampden in the semi-final. Celtic scorers were Lennox, Provan, Doyle, McLeod and McAdam.

JOHN BAXTER (Glasgow) Was Peter Latchford on loan from West Bromwich Albion to Celtic when he won a Scottish Cup medal with them in 1975?

It would appear so. A temporary transfer was arranged on February 19, 1975 and I have no note of its being finalised before the Cup Final on May 3.

TALL ORDER (Glasgow) Details of the Old Firm Scottish Cup tie in the 1950s when Celtic beat Rangers 2-0 after a 4-4 draw.

Teams which drew 4-4 at Parkhead on February 16, 1957 were, CELTIC, Beattie, Haughney, Fallon, Evans, Jack, Peacock, Higgins, Fernie, McPhail, Mochan, Collins.

RANGERS, Niven, Shearer, Caldow, McColl, Davis, Baird, Scott, Simpson, Murray, Morrison, Hubbard.

Scorers were McPhail, Higgins, Collins and Fernie for Celtic and Morrison, Simpson, Hubbard and Murray for Rangers. At Ibrox where the teams were the same, goals by Higgins and Mochan put Celtic through.

CALLING SAVOY BAR (Glasgow)

Celtic team which beat Rangers 5-0 in the semi-final of the 1925 Scottish Cup was, Shevlin, W McStay, Hilley, Wilson, J McStay, McFarlane, Connelly, Gallagher, McGrory, Thomson, McLean.

CHAPTER THREE

Strips
the Green and White Hoops

The hoops evoke so much passion and sentiment that it comes as a shock to realise that this was not the original strip and that around the turn of the century the side came out in green and white vertical stripes.

Gradually the broad green and white hoops took over with their odd effect of increasing the apparent girth of the players so that such as Jimmy McGrory, Jimmy Quinn and Sean Fallon from different decades of the club's history appeared improbably thick-set and squat.

From time to time it was necessary for Celtic to change strips for a league match, although not often since only Hibs were likewise attired in green. Against my own Queen's Park they very often changed since both jerseys contained a lot of white. As boys we were always glad to see this happen as the all-white jerseys with shamrocks or all-green jerseys with shamrocks were nothing like as intimidating. Almost all my recollections of Queen's Park successes against Celtic were when the latter were wearing their change strip. The unease communicated itself to the Celtic support themselves who would groan audibly as their changed team took the field and would assure each other dolefully that "we never do anything in that strip!"

With the coming of European football it became necessary to

identify players positively and Celtic hit upon the unhappy compromise of putting a number on the shorts, useless on a glaury November day after the first ten minutes. When these numbers first appeared in a friendly against Sparta Rotterdam at Parkhead (a match which crops up frequently) there was such an outcry that it might have been supposed to be a crime as serious as drawing a moustache on the face of the Mona Lisa.

Certainly the numbering of a hooped jersey did present peculiar difficulties which on the evidence of visits to Parkhead neither Morton nor Sporting Lisbon had completely solved. In recent years though, Celtic have been given explicit instructions to join the rest of the world.

Questions on strips roll in. What happened to the green and black vertical stripes chosen as the alternate strip in the late 1970s? Answer, quietly forgotten about. Have Celtic goalkeepers ever worn red sweaters? Answer, will find a definite instance. Why do Celtic now wear their away strip in matches where there seems no possible colour clash? Answer, check the contract with the suppliers.

There have been modifications to the hoops in recent years but despite the tendency of the modern player to resemble a walking sandwich board and the vulgarity which sticks chevrons and circles on every vacant inch of space, the Celtic strip still manages to look fresher and more uncluttered than most and gives the phrases "jersey player" and "jersey supporter" real meaning.

STRIPS

GARTCRAIG (Glasgow) My pal says Celtic wore numbered shorts for the first time against Wolves when the floodlights were opened at Parkhead. I say it was later than that and that Sparta Rotterdam were the opponents.

You are right here. The numbers made their first appearance against Sparta Rotterdam in a friendly match played in May 1960.

J.C. (Bridgeton) What was Celtic's strip when they beat Rangers 7-1 in the League Cup final of 1957?

They wore their normal green and white hoops.

P.C. (Baillieston) I'm positive that Liverpool's registered strip around the 1950s was a green and white hooped outfit similar to Celtic's. My friend disagrees.

And so do I. Checking many reference books I can't find any reference to such a jersey, not even as a change strip.

JOHN BAXTER (Glasgow) Celtic changed colours against Airdrie at Parkhead last week (1974). I thought changing was not allowed unless the colours clashed, which Celtic and Airdrie's do not.

As I understand it a team is free to play in its registered alternative strip if there is the slightest possibility of any confusion. The jerseys of both these clubs contain a large amount of white but like yourself I would have thought a change was hardly necessary. It is entirely a matter for clubs and referee.

JACKS (Bridgeton) Please confirm that in Celtic's first home league game of season 1973-74 against Clyde each Celtic player wore the number eight on his shorts. Also give scorers and teams.

This happened in September 1973 and the idea was to commemorate Celtic's eighth consecutive championship. Teams were, CELTIC, Hunter, McGrain, Brogan, Murray, McNeill, Connelly, McLaughlin, Hood, Dalglish, Hay, Lennox.

CLYDE, Cairney, McHugh, Swan, Beattie, McVie, Ahern, Sullivan, Burns, Gillespie, McGrain, Millar.

Celtic won 5-0 and their scorers were McGrain, Dalglish and Lennox (3, 1 pen.).

CHAPTER FOUR

Celtic in the League

It is strange that a side which at three different periods has put four, six and nine consecutive championships together should have gained the reputation of being more suited to the one-off Cup competition. But this has been the case for much of Celtic's history and has been a burr under the skin of the support.

Over the piece Celtic supporters are discerning folk and they know that, especially in Scotland, a Cup can be won without encountering top-flight opposition until the day of the final and perhaps not even then. Therefore the supreme test of merit must be the league with its testing weekly programme and having to meet the chief rivals on hostile ground.

Those who say that figures lie are very often merely attempting to bolster a weak case. No objective observer could deny that Celtic reigned supreme for the first quarter of a century of Scottish League football. Equally, no one could deny that their league record from 1919 to 1965 with six wins in 39 starts was truly appalling and only partly explained by the fact that as late as the 1930s Celtic were struggling along without a reserve side, the falsest of false economies.

Well, what do the readers want to know about this long period in the wilderness? Not the near misses, for there were hardly any.

Opposite
Bobby Lennox in the act of adding another to his tally in a league match against Motherwell in September 1975

Celtic were not infrequently second but rarely took matters absolutely down to the wire. Inquiries are about individual feats, such as scoring six against Rangers and nine against Kilmarnock in 1938-39 but the flag went to Ibrox for all that.

It had not been so before the First World War when acceptance of the title in April seemed as much part of the calendar year as Easter or Christmas. But Celtic grew complacent, Maley grew older, Struth proved a much more formidable foe than any of his predecessors and the long night began.

The inter-war period was tolerable because the Scottish Cup record was good and in the short term that kept the supporters happy. There was at this stage a growing gap between the Old Firm sides and this was accentuated by the war years, which are more fully dealt with elsewhere in the book. The isolated success of 1954 was therefore very welcome, as it ensured such stalwarts as Tully, Fernie, Mochan and Stein of a League medal. Stein's medal was invaluable in enabling him to deflect any criticism in his early days at Dunfermline, footballers being great lads for the "What did you do in the war, daddy?" line of approach.

Nevertheless 1954 was in every sense a false dawn and real success had to await the arrival of the said Stein as manager in 1965 and now the questions also begin to arrive thick and fast. Is it true that of the nine championships none were clinched at Parkhead? Answer, perfectly true – the only one clinched on a home match took place when Celtic were using Hampden Park temporarily. Is it true that only Bobby Lennox and Billy McNeill were there from start to finish? Answer, that is so.

From start to finish one can discern almost three entirely different teams in the course of this record-breaking feat with the two players already named as the constants. Elsewhere Young gave way to Craig, gave way to McGrain and McBride gave way to Wallace gave way to Deans. The first crop of youngsters drifted in, notably Dalglish and Macari and then in the third phase Davidson and Wilson. In stark contrast to the 1930s there was an excellent reserve side known as the Quality Street Kids which produced a seemingly unending supply of talent for the first team.

Everyone remembers the Lions but others deserve to live on in memory, not least Harry Hood, Charlie Gallagher and John Hughes.

Three of the title finishes have been particular cliff-hangers and supporters never tire of writing in about them. The first is the match against Morton at Parkhead on the second-last day of season 1967-68. Morton looked very like hanging on for a goal at Parkhead which would have got them the draw and very probably taken the flag to Ibrox, for news had come through that Rangers had taken a lead late in their game at Rugby Park. It was the old reliable, Bobby Lennox who scrambled the winner in injury time, not the prettiest of goals but then Stein used to say, "Why do you think you always have to score good goals?"

There was the truly heroic win in 1979 when in the last match of the season against Rangers at Parkhead Celtic, down 0-1 and reduced to ten men by the sending off of the late John Doyle, fought back to take the lead at 2-1, survived a Rangers equaliser and went on to win 4-2. And mention has been made elsewhere of the crushing win at Love Street which allowed Celtic to take advantage of Hearts' slip-up at Dundee in 1986

Often of course it is not the last-day dramatic surge which wins the League and an astute query will sometimes throw this up. The question is, "When did Celtic win at Ibrox but fail to win an away game against Rangers? The answer is that same season of 1978-79 when both Rangers home matches were played at Hampden but right at the end of the season. Celtic played St Mirren at Ibrox as work was in progress at Love Street. In the Ibrox match Celtic scored two late-ish goals in a nerve-ridden affair which kept them in contention when Rangers came to Parkhead.

It is a characteristic of the column that ill-wishers, under an affecting guise of concern, will write in seeking negative information about both clubs. There are still those out there who wish to reacquaint themselves with Celtic's 8-0 defeat on Motherwell's ground on April 30 1937. If the devoted follower wants them there were certain extenuating circumstances. The

Steve Chalmers beats keeper McDonald of Falkirk at Parkhead with Willie Wallace in attendance

match was played on a Friday evening to allow Celtic to attend the F A Cup final between Sunderland and Preston North End at Wembley on the next day. Celtic had won the Scottish Cup the previous Saturday and there was an end-of-term feeling about the players. It was hinted delicately and euphemistically that "some of the Celts were not in prime condition."

In addition the goalkeeper Joe Kennaway was injured early in the match and had to hand over the jersey and with another serious injury Celtic finished with nine men. No matter, 8-0 it was and a disgrace by any standards. But it led to one of the most famous stories in the Scottish game. Into Willie Maley's Queen Street restaurant, The Bank, came a man one day who in the course of conversation ungraciously and bravely asked Maley if he remembered this particular match. Maley, to whom the soft word did not easily come, glared at the fellow and roared, "How can I not remember it when buggers like you keep reminding me of it?"

With the 1980s the League took a new direction. Now for a spell the major threat was not Rangers but the so-called New Firm, Aberdeen and Dundee United and in the early 1980s these clubs called the tune with one win to Dundee United and two wins to Aberdeen, Celtic being always "placed" in racing terms and Rangers never in the first three.

That of course changed dramatically with the arrival at Ibrox of Graeme Souness and even more so with the farsighted decision of David Murray to let Walter Smith have his chance when Souness left Rangers for Liverpool. Six years have now elapsed since Celtic last took the title and in those six years they have made nothing that could be considered as a serious challenge.

The patience of the supporters has been legendary but it is not inexhaustible and although any trophy would satisfy short term wants, another championship is essential soon if the new directorate and the new management are to be seen to turn the ship round.

Meanwhile the arguments will continue to wax furious. Would the double team of 1988 have been able to cope with the Lisbon

Lions? Would Jimmy McGrory's 50 goals of 1936 have been overtaken by Joe McBride in 1966-67 but for the latter's severe injury just before Christmas?

These topics are however the raw material of fantasy and as my predecessor, the redoubtable Jaymak was accustomed to growl morosely, "This is a column which deals in facts. We'll have none of your damned speculation here!"

THE SCOTTISH FOOTBALL LEAGUE

THE DRUM BAR (Shettleston) After Celtic arrived home from a game in Russia late on a Friday they played Hearts the following day at Tynecastle. Who played at centre-half for Celtic in this match which Hearts won 3-2 or 4-2?

John Cushley was at centre-half in this match on January 29, 1966 and Hearts winning margin was 3-2.

P.C. 99 (Glasgow) When Celtic were in danger of relegation around 1950 did they beat Dundee 3-1 at Dens Park and did Jock Weir score all the Celtic goals?

At Dens Park on April 17, 1948.

Dundee 2 (Ewen, McKay), Celtic 3 (Weir, 3).

ANGRY ANDY (Glasgow) Could you please tell me the total number of games Celtic have lost in their seven consecutive seasons as league champions? (1966-72)

In their seven championship years Celtic have played 238 league games and lost only 19 of them which is a remarkable record of consistency.

T.M. (Dumbarton) Can you confirm that Jimmy McGrory scored three goals in three minutes against First Division opposition?

He did this against Motherwell at Parkhead on March 14, 1936.

AULD COKER (Camelon) Can you oblige with both teams in the match in which John Thomson was killed?

On September 5, 1931 in a 0-0 draw at Ibrox these were the teams. RANGERS, Dawson, Gray, McAulay, Meiklejohn,

Simpson, Brown, Fleming, Marshall, English, McPhail, Morton.
CELTIC, J Thomson, Cook, McGonagle, Wilson, McStay,
Geatons, R Thomson, A Thomson, McGrory, Scarff, Napier.

BUNBEG (Gweedore) Give the goalscorers when Celtic lost to, and then beat, Dundee United within a week in April 1981.

On April 15, 1981 Celtic lost a Scottish Cup semi-final replay 3-2. United scorers were Bannon, Heggarty and Conroy o.g. with Nicholas (pen) and Provan scoring for Celtic. A week later at Tannadice the score was reversed. This time Pettigrew and Sturrock scored for the home side and McLeod, McGarvey and Burns had the goals which won the Premier Division championship for Celtic.

COLLIE DUG (Glasgow) Please state when the Premier Division was formed and give winners in sequence until now, January 1984. Did Kenny Dalglish win a Premier Division badge with Celtic?

Till the time you mention the Premier Division winners were Rangers, Celtic, Rangers, Celtic, Aberdeen, Celtic, Celtic, and Dundee United. In the league campaign of 1976-77 Kenny Dalglish missed only one match so of course he has a medal.

POSSIL BAR (Glasgow) Did Alan Sneddon win both a Premier and a First Division medal in the same season?

In season 1980-81 he had 15 championship appearances for Celtic and 14 First Division matches for Hibernian. He is therefore entitled to both medals.

BULLIED WEE (Glasgow) Please give the result of the Ne'erday League match of 1975 between Celtic and Clyde.

The game was played at Parkhead, Celtic winning 5-1. Teams were,
CELTIC, Hunter, McGrain, McCluskey, Glavin, McNeill, Connelly, Johnstone, Dalglish, Deans, Callaghan, Wilson.
CLYDE, Cairney, Anderson, John Burns, Ahern, McVie, Jim Burns, Sullivan, Miller, Boyle, Swan, Marshall.
For Celtic Deans, Callaghan (2), Dalglish and Glavin scored with Boyle first-footing for Clyde.

W.E.C. When did John Thomson come to Celtic? What was his

junior club, how many honours did he win and did they include a championship medal?

He came to Celtic in February 1927 from Wellesley Colliery, Fife. With regard to major competitions he had four Scottish caps and two Scottish Cup medals. He never won a League Championship medal.

FORM 10 (Glasgow) What is Celtic's longest undefeated run and how does this compare with Rangers?

Celtic went 63 games without defeat from November 1915 until April 1917. Rangers were unbeaten in 38 consecutive league matches from March 1928 until March the following year.

WILLS (Larbert) What is the most emphatic league win ever recorded by Celtic?

In 1895 they defeated Dundee 11-0 at Parkhead and this is the record margin still for a Scottish League top division game.

J.A.M. (Cambuslang) Please give teams and scorers in the Old Firm league match of September 1961.

This was a 2-2 draw played at Ibrox when the teams were, RANGERS, Ritchie, Shearer, Caldow, Davis, Paterson, Baxter, Scott, McMillan, Christie, Brand, Wilson.

CELTIC, Haffey, McKay, Kennedy, Crerand, McNeill, Price, Chalmers, Jackson, Hughes, Divers, Fernie.

Scorers were Christie and Baxter for Rangers and Divers and Fernie for Celtic.

KNOXY AND DEMI (Yarrows) I say that Paddy Crerand scored an own goal in his last Old Firm match, a 4-0 win for Rangers.

That was certainly the score in the Ne'erday game of 1963 but Rangers scorers were given as Davis, Millar, Wilson and Greig.

SWAIN (Greenock) Were Celtic ever beaten at Port Glasgow when the latter were members of the old First Division?

They were never beaten by Port Glasgow Athletic on the latter's ground. They did however lose the Parkhead match of 1906-07 when Port Glasgow won by a goal to nil.

CHAPTER FIVE

On Goalkeepers

There is no doubt as to the goalkeeper who most strongly rooted himself in the affection of the Celtic supporters. He was John Thomson whose career came to an untimely end at Ibrox on a September afternoon in 1931 when he was killed after an accidental clash with Rangers forward Sam English.

Two characteristics appear to have distinguished Thomson, a courage that bordered almost on the foolhardy, and a particular grace in his movements. Over the years I have asked several of the inter-war players for their opinion of him in comparison with other keepers and almost to a man they have nominated him as the best of his time. From his team mates that might be no more than an estimate born out of loyalty and the passage of time but more interesting is the fact that the famous Queen's Park forward J B McAlpine thought him unexcelled, as did Bob McPhail of Rangers and even more tellingly the great Ibrox keeper Jerry Dawson.

Of the pre-war, that is pre-1914, goalkeepers Davie Adams and Charlie Shaw stand out although it is ironic that Shaw, a fine and durable keeper has gone down as the dupe in the song, "Oh Charlie Shaw, he never saw, where Alan Morton put the ba'." Davie Adams had torn his hand open on a nail in the goalposts while playing in a benefit for a Rangers player at Ibrox. Till his recovery the Ibrox club sportingly offered the use of their reserve goalkeeper, Tom Sinclair and he proved invaluable in his short

spell at Parkhead, playing six league matches without conceding a goal and then winning a Glasgow Cup medal before returning to Ibrox.

After the death of Thomson it took a little while before Celtic found a permanent successor and he attracts queries because he was one of the handful of foreign players in Scottish football at that time. Joe Kennaway, capped not only for Scotland but also Canada and the United States, had a whiff of the exotic about him and he filled the Celtic goal throughout the 1930s, being a bulwark in the great side which took the Scottish Cup in 1937 and the League and the Exhibition Trophy the following season.

Sometimes a player can be unlucky in the time he joined a club. Such was certainly the case with Willie Miller and it is good to see that the older supporter still remembers him with affection. In the years 1942-51 it was his misfortune to play in some of the worst Celtic sides of all time when it was only his skill and courage that kept defeat to respectable proportions (there was seldom any doubt that it would be a defeat).

He particularly excelled in his cutting-out of the cross ball – only Jimmy Cowan compared – and having seen every Celtic goalkeeper since Joe Kennaway, I would have no hesitation in putting him among the top three Celtic goalkeepers of the last sixty years.

Occasionally keepers flashed across the afternoon sky like comets. Such was George Hunter who came from nowhere to claim a place in the 1951 Cup winning side. It was a great sadness when illness curtailed his top-level career but he had the consolation of knowing that nothing protects a player's future reputation more than premature retirement.

In the 1950s Johnny Bonnar had some memorable performances, notably in the Coronation Cup final of 1953 against

Opposite
Minutes to live – John Thomson fists clear a high ball in the Old Firm League clash at Ibrox in September 1931, minutes before the collision with Sam Englsih in which the goalkeeper was fatally injured

Hibernian, without ever absolutely establishing himself. Both Frank Haffey and John Fallon had all the qualities to be really outstanding goalkeepers except perhaps the ideal temperament for the position. Certainly John Fallon was not helped by the fact that Jock Stein's one major weakness was in his approach to goalkeepers. He appeared not to understand the position. Jim Craig, the Lisbon Lion, once memorably said to me that it was his opinion that if Jock had been asked to redesign the game from scratch, he would not have had goalkeepers. Certainly in his time as manager at Parkhead the number of goalkeepers he signed ran into double figures and at least three or four of these could have done a longterm job had their manager left them to get on with it.

Almost irresistibly comic then, that the great goalkeeper of the 1960s should have arrived at Parkhead almost by accident. I deal elsewhere with the myth of Stein and Ronnie Simpson, still guaranteed to bring in a couple of letters a month, as the fans refuse to accept the definite truth. Ronnie Simpson was an astonishing keeper and I write this as one who saw his debut against Clyde as a 14 year old in 1945. As a boy he was spectacular but showy and technically suspect. Over the years he became a marvellous preventive goalkeeper (few who saw it will ever forget his back-heel in the European Cup tie of 1967) and he had the ability to throw the ball to a colleague while still on the way down from having clutched it. No matter how intense the pressure, the defence knew that "Faither was behind them". In the film, *The Celtic Story* there is a wonderful vignette from the 2-2 draw at Ibrox which clinched a league championship. Celtic are attacking and suddenly the camera cuts to Simpson. He is 100 yards from the scene of action yet he prowls up and down his goal-line with his eyes glued to the other end of the park.

He was a hard act to follow and nobody quite succeeded although Alistair Hunter, Denis Connaghan, Evan Williams and

Opposite
One of the bravest and best of all Scottish goalkeepers, Willie Miller, who performed heroically in very bad Celtic sides for almost seven years

Peter Latchford were all good servants of the club. Perhaps had Jock Stein shown more confidence in John Fallon he might well have been the answer.

In another of football's strange twists Jock Stein's very last signing, Paddy Bonner, proved to be a major acquisition and after 16 years in which he has seen off at least half a dozen challengers he has been brought back to Parkhead by the latest manager to take over Celtic, Tommy Burns.

Pat Bonner should have several seasons left. My letter writers think so and know that he can put the bad goal lost against Holland in the World Cup Finals behind him. I remember Ronnie Simpson when 37 being heavily slated for a soft goal he had lost with the undeniable imputation that approaching age was mainly responsible for the lapse. I can still hear Ronnie pointing out calmly and politely that he had often lost just that kind of goal when he was but 18 years old.

Goalkeeping is an attractive and responsible post. It is quite clear that the column's correspondents have not forgotten the engaging enthusiasm of Frank Haffey, the consummate professionalism of Ronnie Simpson and the artistry and astonishing courage of Willie Miller who spent a career plunging at the feet of opponents and of John Thomson who did the same thing once too often.

GOALKEEPERS

MICHAEL C. (Coatbridge) **Who was Hibs goalkeeper about seven or eight years ago when Celtic beat Hibernian 1-0 after extra time in a Scottish Cup replay? I'm betting it was Ronnie Simpson**

Ronnie Simpson was the Hibernian goalkeeper in this quarter-

Opposite
Not what it seems! – the position of Steve Chalmers is a giveaway – Ronnie Simpson is playing for Hibernian and against Celtic in this league match of 1963

final replay at Easter Road on March 15, 1961. John Clark scored the winner in extra time.

ANDERSTON CROSS (Glasgow) Who was Celtic's goalkeeper in their first game after John Thomson's death on September 5, 1931?

He was Johnny Falconer from Cowdenbeath. Falconer had seven league games for Celtic and Joe Coen three, before Joe Kennaway came from the United States to take over.

ARGUMENT (Hillington) Is it true that Celtic had three different goalkeepers in the Scottish Cup Finals of 1911, 1912 and 1914. Please give keepers and backs in these finals.

The 1910-11 back three were Adams, McNair, Hay; in 1912 Mulrooney, McNair, Dodds; and in 1914 Shaw, McNair, Dodds.

JOHN W. (Vancouver) Can you tell the exiled fans out here anything regarding Celtic's new goalkeeper Evan Williams?

Evan Williams, born in Dumbarton, joined Third Lanark from Vale of Leven in October 1964. He went to Wolves in March 1966 and joined Celtic in October 1969.

U.S.A. (Gourock) If Joe Kennaway, the Celtic goalkeeper was capped by Scotland in a Home International match can you date it and give the full Scotland side.

His cap came in a 3-2 defeat by Wales at Cardiff on October 4, 1933 when the Scotland side was, Kennaway (Celtic), Anderson (Heart of Midlothian), Urquhart (Hibernian), Busby (Manchester City), Blair (Motherwell), McLuckie (Manchester City), McGurk (Birmingham), McMenemy, McFadyen (both Motherwell), Easson, (Portsmouth), Duncan, (Derby County). Kennaway also played for Scotland against Austria at Hampden in November 1933.

WOODPECKER (Dumfries) Please list all the senior clubs Ronnie Simpson had. Was he a first-team goalkeeper at Easter Road before joining Celtic?

His clubs in order were Queen's Park, Third Lanark, Newcastle United, Hibernian and Celtic. He was first choice for some time with Hibernian. In season 1963-64 for instance he made 31 league appearances out of a possible 34.

MORTON PIT (Carmyle) When did Charlie Shaw leave Celtic? Did he play for any other senior club afterwards?

Charlie Shaw left Celtic in season 1925-26 and had a few games for Clyde. He had joined Celtic from Queen's Park Rangers, then a Southern League club.

BOBBY THE PLATER (Glasgow) Who was the first to sign as goalkeeper for Celtic, Falconer or Coen?

Coen was the first to sign, in May 1931 as against Falconer's September 1931 but records show Falconer as taking over from the late John Thomson. Joe Coen moved on to Stenhousemuir in March 1932.

SHEEP'S HEAD (Paisley) Who was Celtic's first-ever goalkeeper?

Celtic's goalkeeper in their first official match, a friendly against Rangers which they won 5-2 was Michael Dolan of Drumpellier.

JACKIE (Kilsyth) When and where did Joe Kennaway have his first game for Celtic. Full Celtic team if possible, please.

His first match was against Motherwell at Fir Park on October 17, 1931 when the Celtic team read, Kennaway, Cook, McGonagle, Geatons, McStay, Whitelaw, McGhee, Thomson, Scarff, Napier, Hughes.

W.H.C. (Glasgow) What happened to Jim Foley, the Celtic goalkeeper who played in the New Year's Day match of 1936 when Celtic lost 4-3 at Parkhead?

Best I can do for you is to say that he went to Plymouth Argyle on December 31, 1936 and was put on their open-to-transfer list at a fee of £1500 in May 1938.

ADAMSLIE (Kirkintilloch) Give details of goalkeeper Willie Miller's first appearance for Celtic.

It was in a Southern League match against Hamilton Academical at Parkhead on August 22, 1942. He took over from Jim Culley and from then on was an automatic first-team choice.

CHAPTER SIX

The Managers

The secret of Celtic's success was in their continuity of managership, only four men holding the post in the first 90 years of the club's history. Since then there have been five managerial changes involving four people. But from the point of view of the column (I write as the sixth manager in this period, Tommy Burns, is appointed) there are few or no questions about him or his immediate predecessor, Lou Macari.

Of the managers to date two of them, Jimmy McGrory and Billy McNeill tend to attract rather more questions on their playing careers, rather than their managerial spells. Let us have a look at how the various managers have registered in the consciousness of the fans.

WILLIE MALEY

Willie Maley had a remarkable record in the running of Celtic, being responsible for their fortunes for the 43 years between 1897 and 1940. He was good enough to play twice for Scotland although born in Ireland – residential qualifications were more lax in those early days – but it was as an administrator that he really made his mark. In temperament he bore a marked resemblance to his great rival Bill Struth. Both men were brusque in manner, both totally

Footballing rarity – Willie Maley, approaching his 90th year, kicks off a testimonial match against Bohemians of Dublin at Parkhead

single-minded in their devotion to the fortunes of their respective clubs, both had a great love of athletics. Maley knew himself what it was to win League and Cup medals and he presided over the Celtic teams which took the flag six years in succession from 1905-10 and four years on the trot from 1914-17. He also had a remarkable facility for disguising comparative failure so that between the wars Celtic were only champions in four completely peace-time seasons but somehow still ranked as equals with Rangers in the public perception.

Readers are obviously surprised when they come to tot up the number of forwards he was prepared to let go to England – Charlie Napier, Frank and Hugh O'Donnell, Willie Buchan. And Jimmy McGrory would have followed them if the player had been agreeable to move. He could be peculiarly ungracious to players who had served the team well and at different times the bright sparks such as Patsy Gallagher and Tommy McInally felt the lash of his tongue and the weight of his disciplinary displeasure.

His departure in February 1940, when he was in his 71st year and it might well have seen the natural thing, was badly handled and created great bitterness. In retrospect he should have gone in 1938 when the club's Jubilee Celebrations had been enhanced by the winning of the League championship and the Empire Exhibition Trophy.

As it was he was bundled out of his job in the early months of the war and replaced by Jimmy McStay. Ironically, had Celtic held their hand for a couple of months more their first choice, Jimmy McGrory, would have become available as Kilmarnock closed down for the duration of the war in May 1940. It is fair to say that Maley never recovered from the shock of dismissal and for many years he never went near Celtic Park although some sort of reconciliation took place shortly before he died in his 90th year. Had he been allowed to carry on, and he was still a vigorous man in his early seventies, it is certain that he would not have allowed the directors to adopt the palsied and half-hearted approach to wartime football which they subsequently implemented.

In a pleasant gesture, Rangers invited the ousted chief to attend matches at Ibrox with them and Maley was openly grateful for this gesture. Supporters writing in many years ago had an instinctive understanding of how important Maley had been to their club. From the earliest days he saw the value of matches against foreign opposition so that even before the First World War Celtic had played against sides in the old Austro-Hungarian Empire and between the wars went to the United States. Unusually for a serving manager he was President of the Scottish League between 1921-24.

JIMMY McSTAY

Letters about the second manager are often prompted by a sense of injustice. Was he forbidden to use guest players during the war if they wanted additional payments? Did the club directors state that wartime football did not matter? Did he learn of his own sacking from a newspaper board near Parkhead? Answers are yes, yes and yes.

Jimmy McStay had been a Celtic player of considerable distinction in the late 20s and early 30s, never quite so good perhaps as his brother Willie and certainly never as abundantly honoured in representative football but nevertheless a top-rank First Division player. In his fifteen playing years he won a league medal and five Scottish Cup medals and he had an imposing presence as club captain.

When his playing days were over he spent a short time as player-manager in League of Ireland football before taking over Alloa Athletic. Here he had immediate success, piloting them to promotion in 1939 but the outbreak of war deprived him of the fruits of his success. He moved from Alloa with a good heart in 1940 because he knew the club had decided to close down at the end of the season.

His time at Parkhead was a disaster and all the more hurtful

now you know *about* . . . CELTIC

because it had nothing to do with his personal managerial ability or lack of it. He was faced with a Board which had neither the courage to pull out of wartime football nor the energy to particpate in it seriously. Never in charge in the strict sense, McStay had to watch as the pre-war side was needlessly dispersed and replaced with raw untried recruits from minor grade football who would in any event be called up to the Forces before they could remotely make the transition.

In that situation luck rarely runs your way and McStay must have been close to despair when Jimmy Delaney, one of the three top-class players he had left, missed the better part of two seasons with a bad arm break. By the end of the war it was clear that the directors would make a change when peace came but McStay, short-changed for five years, was denied even the courtesy of being told this to his face. Was he a good manager? One reader summed it up very well. "We will never know, he simply was not given the chance."

JIMMY McGRORY

The replacement for Jimmy McStay was probably the most popular Celtic player of all time up until then (1945). Brave, scrupulously fair, he was held in the highest regard by such opponents as Bob McPhail of Rangers and Jack Harkness of Queen's Park and Hearts. He had an unbelievable scoring record of just over a goal for every league match played, 410 goals in 408 matches.

He was not without managerial experience, he had gone to Kilmarnock early in season 1937-8 and immediately taken them

Opposite
Jimmy McStay with the Scottish Cup in 1931 – his career as manager between 1940-45 was much less successful almost entirely due to lack of backing from the Board

to the final of the Scottish Cup where they lost to East Fife. What seemed to have escaped the general notice is that after Kilmarnock closed down in May 1940 there was nothing for him to manage until the Rugby Park side restarted with a reserve team only in August 1944.

The very qualities which had made Jimmy McGrory so deservedly popular as a player conspired to prevent his being a good manager. His natural courtesy prevented his opposing the chairman Robert Kelly, even when he knew the chairman to be wrong. It was widely and correctly believed that he did not have the final say in team selection and certainly the sides fielded in the Scottish Cup Finals of 1955 and 1956, both of which were lost, could be most kindly described as bizarre.

For five years after the resumption of peace-time football in 1946 Celtic were of no account until winning the Scottish Cup in 1951. Thereafter in fairness, there were some successes, most notably the winning of the Coronation Cup in 1953 and the double the following year. There was too the earthshaking 7-1 League Cup triumph of 1957. But generally the picture was of losses in Scottish Cup Finals even when the Parkhead side were strong favourites, of the lack of any credible challenge in the League, and in the total failure to make any kind of impact in Europe.

Those who believed in the conspiracy theory asserted that Robert Kelly was perfectly happy to have second-rank managers in charge who posed no sort of threat to his control. There is no doubt from my mail bag that many supporters believed this totally.

If that had been the case, the strategy came to an end with the appointment of the next manager, Jock Stein. As the gentlemanly Jimmy McGrory moved among his players, pipe in mouth, saying good-bye to his young side which was for ever promising much and achieving little, the new man entered and from now on things would be very different.

Opposite
Inseparables – Jimmy McGrory and his pipe went everywhere; a magnificent player, he was a very popular manager, although one whose achievements were severely limited

JOCK STEIN

A competent player, but not a very good one. That was Jock Stein's description of himself and it was not said with any sense of mock modesty. His football background had been hard – Albion Rovers and Llanelly provided few of football's frills – but he had come back quite unexpectedly to Parkhead and taken part in the semi-revival of the early and mid-50s. After a spell of coaching he had by great good luck taken himself off to Dunfermline Athletic to learn his trade, and the combination of ambitious provincial club and energetic young manager proved devastating. A short and equally successful period with Hibernian paved the way for a return to Parkhead.

Even today, 16 years after he ceased to manage Celtic Stein attracts as many questions as the other managers combined. The league record alone would have ensured this. In his time Celtic went from the perenially poor relations to being for a decade (a very long time in football terms) undoubtedly the leading Scottish club. And this was to say nothing of the impact made in Europe with two finals in the European Cup in the space of four years.

The supporters loved his swashbuckling approach, victory for them has never been over-highly prized unless achieved with style. Possibly not one in a hundred would realise that the nine in a row was achieved with what was in effect three different teams with only Billy McNeill and Bobby Lennox as constants. They loved the way he stood up to his chairman, to the SFA, to anyone, where the interests of Celtic were at stake. Now Celtic were European news, the opinions of their players and officials respected from one end of the Continent to the other.

For a brief while, the ageing ground in the East End of Glasgow became the football capital of Europe as McNeill and Clark held top European attacks at bay, Craig and Gemmell raided piratically, Murdoch, Auld and Johnstone tore defences to tatters and Chalmers and Lennox administered the *coup de grace* on countless occasions.

The king is dead! – Jock Stein looks on ruefully as chairman Desmond White introduces Billy McNeill as the new Celtic manager; the picture of Sir Robert Kelly looks down on the passing of an era

From time to time a crisis was surmounted. Jock decided to stay when it seemed that Manchester United beckoned. He was fortunate to survive a horrific car crash. And yet it ended in tears or near enough and the episode showed how hard it is even for the greatest of managers to part amicably with a club. In 1977-78 Celtic had had a bad season and Rangers who were fast catching up had appointed John Greig who was idolised by the support. Perhaps panicking somewhat, Celtic reacted by placing the equally revered Billy McNeill in charge.

Stein was out and on the day I thought of something he had once said to me in answer to my question. "It's probably a mistake to stay too long anywhere in football. You are maybe still saying the right things but they'll have stopped listening." He was offered, in a bungled way, a place on the board, appeared to accept and then thought better of it. On reflection, it was probably an error even to have made the offer. Inevitably the presence of such a Titan as a director could have made life unnecessarily hard for the new manager, no matter who he was.

He was beloved by the Celtic support who in addition to his many real qualities invested him with some supernatural powers which he did not have as we shall see in our section on myth. Few people, if indeed anyone at all, have so changed the state of the game in Scotland single-handedly by the sheer weight of their personality and intellect. Stein would have been surprised to see the word intellect used in connection with himself but he had one of the most powerful intelligences I have ever encountered. He claims an odd double, the least distinguished player ever to have managed Celtic and by far their most distinguished manager.

BILLY McNEILL

More than twenty years have passed since Billy McNeill last pulled on a Celtic jersey yet he remains one of the great folk heroes. This is hardly astonishing when the indelible image fans have of him is of his receiving one trophy or another and brandishing it aloft, most memorably of course the European Cup in Lisbon in 1967.

His playing career was remarkable, meeting with virtually no tangible success for its first seven years and then winning everything in sight for the remaining ten. He was a dominant driving skipper who looked like a captain. He was a hard but fair competitor, given to refereeing the game for the official but it is a considerable tribute to him that occupying possibly the most physical of all positions, that of centre-half, he had but one sending-off in a long career at top level. He further endeared himself to the support by his agreeable habit of scoring his goals in cup finals, two in the last stages of the Scottish Cup and one in the League Cup final. His first Scottish Cup goal was the winner against Dunfermline Athletic in 1965 and it could be argued very plausibly that it was that goal which turned the whole future of Celtic round.

When he was asked to assume the mantle of Jock Stein he had been away from the playing side for about three years and had been learning the craft of managership with Clyde and Aberdeen. He would agree that with hindsight the offer of the Celtic job perhaps came a little too early in his career. Despite that his record at Parkhead was anything but negligible. In his two spells as manager he won four championships, three Scottish Cups and a League Cup and this included the great centenary double of 1988.

That, in any other circumstances, would have been a genuinely splendid record. But as a supporter wrote to me at the time, "How can anyone be asked to do a job where the definition of success is now ten in a row?" In addition he had to contend with a fast-reviving Rangers and the fact that the deaths of Robert Kelly and Desmond White had deprived Celtic of a dominant presence both at club level and at League and SFA level.

Not that McNeill's relationship with Desmond White had been uniformly harmonious and indeed the end of his first term at Parkhead came in acrimonious circumstances. Following a disagreement over contractual terms, the manager took great exception to the club's revealing details which he had assumed to be confidential.

He moved off to England where he was comparatively unsuccessful with Manchester City and Aston Villa. His recall to Parkhead in 1987 was something of a surprise although a very gratifying one to the support as a whole, as my postbag then would bear witness. As mentioned earlier he guided the side to a notable double in 1988 but increasingly Celtic were bobbing in the Ibrox wake and as time went by and Rangers monopolised the league and began again to acquire the habit of taking the League Cup, there could be only one ending. The parting of the ways from a weak and ineffectual board took place in 1991. Of his commitment to Celtic there was never the remotest doubt. Rarely in the modern era he was a one-club player. He turned out for Celtic more than 800 times and the supporters do not forget him.

DAVID HAY

With the appointment of David Hay as successor to Billy McNeill, Celtic continued the policy of having a former player in charge. David Hay figured in the second of the three separate teams which figured in the nine in a row triumph and to a limited extent he combined the virtues of Bobby Murdoch and John Clark.

He was perhaps the first major indication that things were beginning to go wrong at Parkhead when he moved to Chelsea over a money disagreement in 1974. His going was a severe loss because not only did Celtic lose a player who was a ready-made long-term captain, but with the departure of David Hay went the last hope that George Connelly might have a future at top-level.

Opposite
David Hay followed in the tradition of appointing a distinguished former player as manager and he was in charge during the dramatic last-gasp league title win of 1986

An eye injury had curtailed his playing career in the south and he became first of all assistant manager with Motherwell before taking sole charge. Courteous and usually calm and laid-back, his relaxed demeanour occasionally conveyed the impression that there were more important things in football and this did not always sit well with a support which had been brought up on the driving tactics of Stein and McNeill.

Under his command Celtic won a Scottish Cup and a League championship but the latter was one of the great triumphs of the club's history. A revitalised Hearts had led the championship for the great part of the 1986 season and found themselves in a position on the last day of the season where a draw would ensure the championship for them. Celtic could only run up a large score at Paisley and hope for the best.

Celtic fulfilled their part of the bargain admirably, having the game won at half-time but of course that meant nothing in isolation. Late in the second-half a mad shout of joy from the Love Street terracings announced that Dundee had taken the lead, to be followed by another such shout a few minutes later.

This continues to be one of the half-dozen matches of which details are most often requested but I remember it for another reason. It was Graeme Souness's first match in charge of Rangers and they were playing Motherwell at Ibrox. When the second Dundee goal was scored there was a blaze of joy from the various stands, totally baffling until it emerged that the BBC radio commentator had accidentally credited the goal to Walter, rather than Albert Kidd and the Rangers support believed that Hearts had salvaged the draw which would have been good enough to have given them the title. When the mistake was rectified the cheering stopped with a suddenness as if a giant had wiped a cloth along the front of the stands.

But Souness was to show soon that he had the measure of Celtic. In the short term the manager of the trailing club pays for that and Hay's departure paved the way for the return of Billy McNeill and the beginning of a Magic Roundabout for Celtic managers.

LIAM BRADY

The Now You Know column is a column of fact rather than opinion and over its many years the writers of it have tried to keep it that way. Yet many of the letters which come in about Liam Brady are really heartfelt cries as to why the appointment of a player with such an impeccable pedigree should have gone so wrong.

The correspondents ideas are interesting. There are those of course who are sure they have the reason. Liam Brady never played for Celtic. Ask them if Matt Busby or Alec Ferguson ever played for Manchester United and a heavy silence ensues. More credible perhaps is the view of others that never having played in Scotland he did not know who was good or available or both. This was compounded by the fact that no effort seemed to be made to give power to an assistant manager who did know the Scottish scene.

In all of this of course there is a large element of second-guessing. All fans pick the right side every week and make all the necessary signings. It has to be said that the appointment of Brady was universally well received for he seemed to have the impeccable playing pedigree and reputation that was needed.

It is interesting to reflect that he got the job in preference to Ivan Golacs who later steered Dundee United to their first-ever Scottish Cup success and certainly Golacs did seem to be an infinitely better judge of a player. All managers, even the greatest, sign players who do not make it. If proof of that is needed the reader is again referred to the list of goalkeepers enrolled by Jock Stein.

Some of Liam Brady's signings were not only hideously expensive but hideously inept. It is hard to imagine that anyone seriously thought that such players as Tony Cascarino and Stuart Slater had any real hope of turning Celtic around. Had the board themselves not been under pressure Liam Brady might well have survived but he felt the task to be beyond him and submitted his resignation.

There followed the strange interlude of Lou Macari with most letter-writers feeling that he was never a sufficiently visible presence but a strong minority feeling that in the disturbed boardroom circumstances of the time he got less than a fair chance. Some point to the draw secured at Ibrox in the notorious supporterless game as a considerable achievment.

And now, as this is written, the club has installed another much-admired former player, Tommy Burns. It will be interesting to see what the letters will say about this some ten years from now. The problems faced will be enormous. Breaking the column's normal rule about fact and comment, there are correspondents out there who think that the problem is four managers in the last three years as opposed to four in the first ninety.

THE CELTIC MANAGERS

DICK (Fauldhouse) In which game did Jock Stein, playing for Celtic, have an ankle broken? I say it was against Rangers at Parkhead.

Jock Stein was injured (although there is no mention of a broken ankle) against Rangers at Celtic Park on August 31, 1955. As he played the whole of the second half at outside-left a broken ankle seems unlikely. He resumed in September and had several league games before the end of the season.

CEDARWOOD (Glasgow) When did Jock Stein have his very last game for Celtic and please give the opposition and teams in his last league game?

His very last match was in Ireland against Coleraine on May 17, 1956. The last league game was against Dundee at Parkhead on March 17 when Celtic won 1-0. Teams were, CELTIC,

Opposite
Liam Brady was a brilliant player but his tenure of office at Parkhead was a signal failure, perhaps because of turbulence in the Board Room and his own lack of first-hand knowledge of the Scottish game

Beattie, Haughney, Fallon, Evans, Stein, Peacock, Collins, Fernie, Sharkey, Smith, Tully.

DUNDEE, Brown, Gray, Irvine, Gallacher, Black, Cowie, Stables, Henderson, Merchant, O'Hara, Chalmers.

TENNANT'S (Glasgow) Did Jock Stein pick Scotland's teams against Italy in the World Cup matches in 1965?

As I understand it, Jock Stein, although in temporary charge of the Scottish international team had full say in the choice of team for both matches. He did however express profound dissatisfaction with the system after the 3-0 reverse in Italy when there were many call-offs.

JIMMY B (Barrhead) When did Jimmy McGrory play his last match for Celtic and when did he become manager of Kilmarnock?

Jimmy McGrory's last match for Celtic was against Queen's Park at Celtic Park on October 16, 1937. He accepted the Kilmarnock post in December of that same year.

ROCK BAR (Possilpark) For how long was Jimmy McStay manager of Celtic?

He was appointed manager of Celtic on February 15, 1940 and resigned in July 1945 to be immediately succeeded by Jimmy McGrory.

PARADISE (Glasgow) When Jock Stein signed for Albion Rovers who was their manager? Did he leave Albion Rovers on a free transfer?

Webber Lees was the manager of Albion Rovers when Jock Stein signed for them in 1942. I understand that when he went to Llanelly a nominal fee was involved.

TIM (Scotstoun) I say that as a player Billy McNeill scored two goals against Rangers.

That is correct. The two occasions were in a 4-0 win at Ibrox in a Glasgow Cup tie of 1966 and in the Scottish Cup Final of 1969 when the score was identical.

JOHN BANNON (Glasgow) I know about Jock Stein's successes as a manager but what honours did he win as a player?

He won a Charity Cup medal and a Coronation Cup medal in

1953. *The following year he had a league and cup double and in 1955 a Glasgow Cup medal. In 1954 he played for the Scottish League against the Football League.*

CURIOUS (Govan) How many times did Celtic win the Scottish League, the Scottish Cup, the Glasgow Cup and the Glasgow Charity Cup while Willie Maley was managing them?

During his control from 1888-1940 they won 19 league championships, 15 Scottish Cups, 19 Glasgow Cups and 23 Charity Cups.

OLD TIMER (Tollcross) Can you say when Mr James Kelly, father of Sir Robert, was Celtic chairman and for how long Tom White held this position?

James Kelly was Celtic chairman from 1909-14 when he was succeeded by Tom White who held the position until 1947.

GREEN (Greenock) Can you tell us if Jimmy McGrory ever managed Kilmarnock and if so was it only in war-time football?

His career at Rugby Park was odd. He took over in December 1937 so had a season and a half of normal football. Then followed a year of wartime football before Kilmarnock closed down for four years. From 1944-45 they operated a reserve side only and then McGrory returned to Celtic.

J. DUNCAN (Blackpool) Please give details of Jock Stein's results as manager against Rangers from his taking over until now (June 1973).

In this period 36 matches were played between the two teams, Celtic winning 20 to Rangers 9 with the remaining 7 being drawn. These figures only relate to League, League Cup, Scottish Cup and Glasgow Cup.

MRS MAXWELL'S BAR (Laurieston) Who was Jock Stein's first signing as manager of Celtic?

His first signing was Joe McBride from Motherwell in the summer of 1965.

N0. 10 BAR (Kilmarnock) Did Jimmy McGrory of Celtic ever play for Kilmarnock?

Jimmy McGrory went to Kilmarnock half-way through the 1937-38 season but Celtic retained his playing registration in case he should turn out for Killie. All Jimmy McGrory's playing was done for Celtic except for a season at the outset of his career when he was on loan to Clydebank.

OLD FIRM FANS (Glasgow) Can you tell us if, as things stand today (1974), Celtic shareholders get any dividends or does all the money go to charity when profits are made?

From time to time the club makes charitable donations but shareholders receive dividends in the ordinary way when finances allow.

CROWWOOD HOUSE (Chryston) Was Billy McNeill manager of Celtic when Frank McGarvey was transferred from Liverpool to Parkhead?

Yes. Taking up office on May 28, 1978 he was manager for a few days before this particular transfer.

A. SPIERS (Kilbarchan) Did Billy McNeill take over as manager at Parkhead before John Greig became manager of Rangers?

No, John Greig was senior by four days, taking up his managerial position on May 24, 1978.

ALLIANCE STAFF (Rutherglen) Did David Hay ever captain a Scotland side?

He led out a Scottish team on two occasions. The first was a World Cup qualifying match against Czechoslovakia at Bratislava in October 1973 when Scotland lost 1-0. The second match was a friendly against West Germany in Frankfurt in 1974.

THE NEW CAMPERS (Glasgow) How many goalkeepers did Jock Stein sign as manager of Celtic?

The list is long and includes Tom Livingston, Pat Lally, Evan Williams, Alistair Hunter, Denis Connaghan, Bobby Wraith, Graeme Barclay, Bent Martin, Gordon Marshall, Roy Baines and Peter Latchford. There may be one other that I have missed.

HERBIE (Glasgow) How many first-team games did Ronnie Simpson play before Jock Stein became manager?

Before Stein, Simpson had made 10 appearances, eight in the league and two in the Fairs Cities Cup.

THE WAVERLEY (Glasgow) For how long were Struth and Maley Old Firm managers?

Struth ran Rangers from 1920-53 and Maley was in charge of Celtic officially from 1892-1940.

SOUTH STREET (Glasgow) What were the respective records of Bill Struth and Jock Stein as managers?

Not sure that it is a very meaningful comparison, given the different competitions available to the two men and the differing length of time that they were in their respective posts. In 34 years at Ibrox Struth won 18 championships, 10 Scottish Cups and 2 League Cups. In 13 years at Parkhead Jock Stein won 10 championships, 8 Scottish Cups, 6 League Cups and the European Cup which of course was not an option in Bill Struth's time.

PUB ARGUMENT (Dennistoun) Who signed Jim Melrose for Celtic – David Hay or Billy McNeill?

David Hay had taken over as Celtic manager when Jim Melrose came to Celtic from Leicester City.

CHAPTER SEVEN

Attendances, Floodlights and Ground

The vast majority of football clubs have led a semi-nomadic existence and have shifted quarters several times before what he Victorians charmingly called "the avaricious encroachments of the building fiend". Indeed even in recent years some half-dozen Scottish clubs either have relocated or are in the process of doing so.

Apart from an early move of some few hundred yards Celtic have always been where they are, although the ground has inevitably changed shape with the years. In its time it has hosted boxing matches, speedway racing or dirt-track riding, as it was then known, and religious meetings. Above all, in the early years of this century it had the great cement cycle track to stage meetings of what was almost the most popular sport of its day.

That monument to private enterprise, the Grant Stand, had gone by the late 1920s. Ahead of its time in being heavily glassed, it was essentially unsuitable because that same glass steamed up and obscured visibility. By 1929 the present main stand gave a certain air of authority to the ground which was offset by the ramshackle enclosure on the other side with its sieve-like Dutch barn roof.

"When did the enclosure begin to be called the Jungle?" comes the question. I have found this almost impossible to date with any certainty but I have found no elderly supporter to say that this term was in use before war came in 1939. So was it the Celtic support themselves, in a wry reference to the hardship of the spectating conditions? Or was it a snide reference by visiting supporters to the conduct of its inhabitants?

Those who wish to catch me out, and there are many, often slip in the query, "When was the first floodlit match to be played at Celtic Park?" If they are Israelites in whom there is no guile, then they accept the straightforward answer of October 1959 against Wolves. If of a more historical turn of mind they will know for example that Clyde certainly played at Parkhead under Wells light as far back as 1893.

The more astute will already have registered that 1959 was comparatively late for the introduction of floodlights. Falkirk for example had had them since 1953 and the Edinburgh grounds were also well ahead. The delay was not necessarily a fault because mistakes elsewhere were avoided and the system at Parkhead was very fine. Certainly bright enough to light up the blushes of the home team as they lost to a Wolves side of which half were reserves. Still, the lights were to prove their worth in the great European nights of the 1960s when one of the absolutely unforgettable sporting experiences was to walk out from town on the evening of a European tie and suddenly see the lights blazing into the night sky.

Attendances are much more difficult to quantify. To be sure Celtic have set records at many away grounds. Certainly they have for all time the record attendance for a European Cup tie, upwards of 134,000 for the second leg of the semi final against Leeds United in 1970. I say "upwards of 134,000" deliberately, not out of sloth, but because a gate was broken down that night and nobody has the remotest idea to within 2000 or so how many people actually gained admission.

Readers constantly seek information on attendances and love being told that there were 146,433 spectators at the Aberdeen Cup Final of 1937. Again, a gate was knocked in and the official attendance is, as the scientists used to say, "correct to the nearest bucketful".

No harm done, provided the traditional grain of salt is prominently displayed on the table. Bear in mind that for many years there was no obligation for clubs to disclose League attendances and of course in the very beginning there were no turnstiles capable of recording attendances with any semblance of accuracy. Newspaper estimates of the crowd, until quite recently, were decided by the collective wisdom of the press box. As many press boxes were on the roof of a stand and the stand interior was not visible from the press box the estimation of the crowd was by guess and by God.

The top figure for Celtic Park, 92,000 for the Ne'erday game of 1938 is particularly suspect and was probably 10,000 less than that. This doesn't affect the ones that are rock solid, such as the 120,000 plus that saw the friendly with Real Madrid in the Bernabeu Stadium in the Spanish capital. The lowest attendance would appear to be the 1000 souls who turned up in foul weather for a match against the Paisley side Abercorn in the very earliest days of the Scottish League, but read the preceding cautions before laying money on it.

The threatened move to Cambuslang revived interest in the history of the ground and the number of questions to me on this subject increased. It provided proof that football is essentially about sentiment and the supporters clearly and genuinely believed that, like another ageing and shabby institution Carnegie Hall in New York City, the ground was "a palace of dreams and a temple to the arts."

ATTENDANCES, FLOODLIGHTS AND GROUND

ALEX G. (Glasgow) What was the crowd limit when Celtic met Liverpool in the Cup Winners Cup at Parkhead in 1966?
The crowd limit for this tie, played on April 14 was 80,000.

J.Q. (Drumchapel) When were floodlights first installed at Parkhead and what was the opening match?

The first floodlight game was against Wolves on October 12, 1959.

J. D. (Hunterhill, Paisley) Did the Celtic pavilion ever stand on the Jungle side of the ground?

The Celtic pavilion was at the Gallowgate end of the Jungle side from 1892 until the new stand was opened in 1929.

TAM K (Dundee) I say that during the Second World War there was an Old Firm match at Parkhead when the attendance was only 15,000 by magistrates regulation. Can you date this match and give the score?

You have the wrong venue as the match was held at Hampden Park on September 29, 1941 and was a Glasgow Cup semi-final. Rangers won 3-2 and the all-ticket crowd of 15,000 was on the recommendation of the then Chief Constable of Glasgow, Percy Sillitoe.

JOE (Parkhead) Please give the attendance and scorer when Celtic beat Real Madrid in the Di Stefano benefit game in Madrid.

On June 7, 1967 120,000 people saw Celtic defeat Real Madrid by virtue of a Bobby Lennox goal.

CELTIC SUPPORTER (Irvine) In seasons 1967-68 or 1968-69 did Celtic average a home crowd over the season of 44,000?

No, their best average gate was 34,000 in season 1968-69 but this is very high by Scottish standards.

JAZZA (Castlemilk) Please provide me with the following information. What is the record attendance at Parkhead and what is the present capacity? (1973)

The record attendance at Parkhead was 92,000 against Rangers on January 1, 1938 and the 1973 capacity was 80,000 of whom 4800 were seated.

TEXO (Stirling) When was the Grant stand opened at Celtic Park?

It was opened on October 28, 1899 but was never popular because of bad ventilation which caused the interior of the large glass windows to steam up.

FITBA' DAFT (Glasgow) Have Celtic played to the largest crowds in Scottish Cup Finals, League Cup finals, European Cup matches and any football match in Britain?

The answer is yes to all categories except the last. The largest crowd in British football history was that which attended the 1937 international at Hampden between Scotland and England and the attendance of over 149,000 that day will now never be surpassed.

DAN (Scotstoun) Give the teams and scorers when Celtic played Wolves to celebrate the opening of the Parkhead floodlights.

The match was played on October 12, 1959 with Wolves winning 2-0. Teams were, CELTIC, Fallon, McKay, Mochan, Smith, Evans, Peacock, Chalmers, McVittie, Lochead, Divers, Auld.

WOLVERHAMPTON WANDERERS, Finlayson, Kelly, Harris, Clamp, Stuart, Kirkham, Mason, Durant, Murray, Broadbent, Horne.

Scorers for Wolves were Broadbent and Murray.

CHAPTER EIGHT

Celtic and the League Cup

The League Cup provides a strange facet of Celtic's history. On the one hand it has seen two outstanding triumphs, the 7-1 victory over Rangers in the final of 1957 and the five successes in a row between 1965 and 1969. In general though it has been a tournament in which advantages have not been pressed home. It was 11 years into the competition before Celtic's first appearance in the final and while they were then very good at getting into finals, their record was pretty dismal once there with only 9 successes in 20 appearances.

The question that crops up beyond all others is of course the demands for details about the final of 1957. In a sense of course it is not a question at all since 90% of those who write in are already informed of the match in pitiless detail and simply like to see those details in print. What is remarkable about that match is that at least three of the side made a brief although definite impact at Celtic Park. John Donnelly, Sammy Wilson and Billy McPhail flitted brightly across the East End sky and then were gone.

Still, questions on the match pour in and are followed as night follows day by enquiries from further west in the city seeking assurances that the 8-1 win at Ibrox of Rangers on January 1st 1943 was not imaginary. It is important to pay genuine tribute to Celtic's real achievments in this competition. Their displays in taking five goals off a very good Dundee side and six from an even better Hibernian on at the final stage, rank among the very

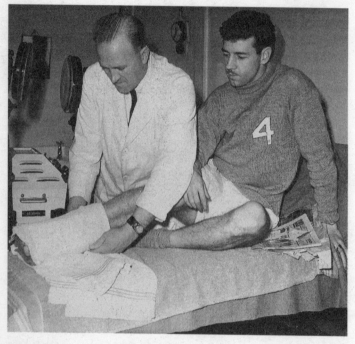

Am I fit for Saturday? – Billy McPhail, star of the famous League Cup Final of 1957 and brother of the popular John, receives treatment from trainer Willie Johnstone

Opposite
Built for comfort not speed! – the inimitable Charlie Tully jogs round Celtic Park in the course of a not-too-strenuous training session

best performances in that competition's history. So too does that marvellous feat of consistency which saw them appear in 14 consecutive finals between 1964 and 1977. At the time of the five successive wins Celtic were sweeping everything out of the way and perhaps those spectators who saw a first minute goal from Bertie Auld dispose of St Johnstone had become a little blasé. They would have done well to cherish it because the subsequent 24 finals have brought only two Celtic successes.

Naturally there are vivid memories. They include the head-flicks of Billy McPhail that destroyed the Rangers defence in 1957, John Hughes scoring twice coolly from the penalty spot in 1965, and the demolition of Hibernian referred to above.

But then as suddenly as they had acquired it, Celtic lost the knack of winning League Cup Finals. For years I was puzzled by the number of Celtic fans who had a compulsive and masochistic desire to be informed of the 4-1 thrashing by Partick Thistle in 1971 until I noticed that most of the letters originated from the North West of Glasgow. This set off a period in which Celtic lost to sides they were expected to beat comfortably. There was nothing quite as dramatic as the 4-0 half-time deficit against Partick Thistle but Hibernian probably should have been beaten in 1972 and, given the respective strengths of the sides, Dundee certainly should have been the following year.

If a poll were taken among the fans, the Dundee match would rank very high in the list of disappointments. Because of the miners' strike the match kicked off just after mid-day and was played on a slushy pitch without the benefit of floodlights. Dundee approached it with more appetite and deserved their win and at the end of it all the only smiling Celtic face was that of Tommy Gemmell, who had by that time moved on to Dundee.

But of course a League Cup is not only about final ties and Celtic players have done remarkable feats at an earlier stage of

Opposite
Ireland's own – Bertie Peacock, an inspirational left-half and a distinguished Northern Ireland international

the competition. In season 1968-69 Bobby Lennox twice scored five goals in the early rounds, and in one of those matches, against Hamilton Academicals, he was joined in going nap by Steve Chalmers. In the qualifying stages Celtic have beaten Rangers twice at Ibrox in the same season and Harry Hood has had an Old Firm semi-final hat-trick.

At the time of going to print it is eleven years since Celtic last tasted League Cup success. It is an important competition to win, it takes pressure off the manager and of course guarantees entry to Europe at an early stage. It is a trophy held in regard by the fans because they associate it with the free-flowing, free-scoring days of such as Joe McBride, Bobby Lennox, Willie Wallace and Stevie Chalmers. It has also, up until now, been the exception to the rule that if Celtic get to a final in any competition, they will finish the job.

THE LEAGUE CUP

GARWALD (Cardross) Can I have the Celtic team that beat Rangers 7-1 in the 1957 League Cup Final plus Celtic's scorers?
The Celtic side was, Beattie, Donnelly, Fallon, Fernie, Evans, Peacock, Tully, Collins, McPhail, Wilson, Mochan. Scorers for Celtic were McPhail (3), Mochan (2), Wilson and Fernie (pen.) with Simpson scoring for Rangers.

SNODDY'S BAR (Paisley) When Bobby Lennox equalised for Celtic against Hibernian in a League Cup semi-final did the game go into extra time?
Bobby Lennox's last-minute equaliser, making the score 2-2 meant that the game went into extra time after which the score was unchanged.

SPARKS (Glasgow) Who was the referee who awarded Celtic two penalty kicks against Rangers in a League Cup Final about 1966? I say it was Hugh Phillips, my pal says Tiny Wharton.
This was the League Cup Final of 1965-66 which Celtic won 2-1 and the referee was Hugh Phillips as you say.

ALLY'S PUB (Kilmarnock) Please give the times and scorers in both games of the League Cup semi-final of 1969 when Celtic beat Ayr United 2-1 after a 3-3 draw.

In the first match Hughes (41), Gemmell (pen.50) and Auld (98) netted for Celtic, Rough (32, 95) and McCulloch (54) doing likewise for Ayr. In the replay Hood (22) and Chalmers (53) were one too many for Ingram (14).

BRIG O'DON (Glasgow) Give teams and score in the 1976 League Cup final between Celtic and Aberdeen. Did it go to extra time, and who was Aberdeen's manager at the time?

Aberdeen, managed by Ally MacLeod, won 2-1 after extra time. Teams were, ABERDEEN, Clark, Kennedy, Williamson, Smith, Garner, Miller, Sullivan, Scott, Harper, Jarvie, Graham.

CELTIC, Latchford, McGrain, Lynch, Edvaldson, MacDonald, Aitken, Doyle, Glavin, Dalgish, Burns, Wilson.

Scorers for Aberdeen were Jarvie and Robb (who substituted for Jarvie) and Dalglish, pen. for Celtic.

MARYHILL JAG (Glasgow) Details please of the 1956 League Cup final between Celtic and Partick Thistle including times when the goals were scored .

Celtic won 3-0 after a goalless draw. Teams in the replay were, CELTIC, Beattie, Haughney, Fallon, Evans, Jack, Peacock, Tully, Collins, McPhail, Fernie, Mochan.

PARTICK THISTLE, Ledgerwood, Kerr, Gibb, Collins, Crawford, Mathers, McKenzie, Wright, Hogan, McParland, Ewing.

The goals, all sandwiched between the 49th and 55th minutes were scored by McPhail (2), and Collins. Celtic were unchanged but in the first match Davidson had been at centre-half and Smith at centre-forward for Thistle.

FOOTBALL FAN (Glasgow) Please give all relevant information on the 1967 League Cup Final between Celtic and Dundee. Did Jim McLean play for Dundee?

Celtic won this 5-3 and Jim Mclean not only played but scored. CELTIC, Simpson, Craig, Gemmell, Murdoch, McNeill, Clark, Chalmers, Lennox, Wallace, Auld, Hughes.

DUNDEE, Arrol, R Wilson, Houston, Murray, Stewart, Stuart, Campbell, J McLean, S Wilson, G McLean, Bryce.

Celtic scorers were Chalmers (2), Wallace, Lennox and Hughes. The McLeans did all the scoring for Dundee with two for George and one for Jim.

PIPESHOP EDDIE (Glasgow) In the late 1960s Celtic beat Morton 7-1 in a League Cup semi-final match. Was the match played on a Saturday or in midweek?

The match was played at Hampden on Wednesday October 11, 1967. Scorers were Hughes (2), Craig (2), Wallace, Lennox and Johnstone for Celtic and Arentoft for Morton. I cannot immediately trace Jim Craig scoring two goals in any other competitive match.

LOW GREEN (Strathaven) Does Bertie Auld have a Football League Cup medal as well as Scottish League Cup medals?

Yes. He was in the Birmingham side which defeated Aston Villa 3-1 on aggregate in the competition of 1962-63.

CHAPTER NINE

Myth and Legend

Your really devoted football follower is a true sentimentalist at heart. That is why we go to matches, to see the club our fathers supported or perhaps the one that an uncle and grandfather played for. Sometimes the sentiment goes beyond the bounds of reality and both sets of Old Firm fans cherish curious notions of what they think happened, holding these views so strongly that no amount of telling them it wasn't so will convince them.

The King Arthur of the Celtic story is Jock Stein, a man whose actual achievments were so monumental that it might be thought no legend could embellish them. But for many he has to be credited with the supernatural foresight of sending Ronnie Simpson on ahead to Parkhead from Easter Road because he knew he himself would be following him. The reality is duller. The two had never hit it off at Easter Road and the manager thought the 34 year old goalkeeper was swiftly nearing the end of his career. Ronnie himself has said that when the news of Stein's appointment to Parkhead was flashed up on the television screen his immediate reaction was to shout through to his wife in the kitchen, "Pack your bags, we're on the move again!"

And yes, all the rest, the injury and loss of form by John Fallon, the European Cup medal and the first cap at the age of almost 37, all were sheer chance. Not nearly as good a story maybe, but the way it was.

Nor did Jock Stein, contrary to popular legend wear a tattoo of King Willam III on his chest, nor still less did he declare after Lisbon in 1967 that the Lions would never play together again so that they would remain for all time undefeated after their European Cup success.

In actual fact they played together on at least two or three occasions in the following season, losing certainly one of their matches to Dundee United. Partly these stories have arisen from Stein's considerable gifts as showman for he was entitled to a PRO's salary from Celtic in addition to his managerial payment. Who else could have hit on the idea of spicing up a meaningless game against Clyde by announcing that for the very last time the Lisbon side would take the field together although it was well-known that Ronnie Simpson could not possibly play? It was the same P T Barnum quality that led him to send out the whole eleven with number eight on their shorts at the start of the new season after the eighth title win in succession.

The last parade of the Lions and the number eight shorts did happen however, unlike the happy scenario which imagines John and Billy McPhail in the same Celtic side. They only missed each other by three weeks, it is true, but three weeks was enough.

Charlie Tully likewise would have been ecstatic had he played on a winning Irish side at Wembley and in the process scored direct from a corner-kick against the giant English goalkeeper Frank Swift. But Charlie did not accomplish either of these deeds.

Occasionally questions which ought to be mythical turn out to be true. Such as, "Is it the case that Jimmy McGrory never played for Scotland at Wembley?" That ought to be the stuff of legend given that in over 400 games McGrory averaged more than a goal a game. But it is alas, only too true.

But then, goalscoring centre-forwards never had much chance with the Scottish selectors. Ask Henry Morris of East Fife who, called to the colours in 1950 against Northern Ireland, scored three of our goals, eight in all, only to find that his services were never again required.

Some hardy annuals are just plain daft. Did Celtic go through a season before the First World War, Adams in goal, when they lost only one single goal in a league campaign. You will not be astonished to learn that the answer is no.

Deeply rooted in the Celtic soul is the conviction that crucial decisions go against them, particularly in Old Firm matches and even more in the awarding of penalty kicks. As an exercise I looked in the early 1980s at the total number of penalties awarded to each side in such matches and what I found was surprising and interesting.

By that time the sides had been playing each other for five years short of the century and yet the discrepancy in penalty kicks over that very long period was a mere five in Rangers favour. But there was another, more notable discrepancy and it was this. Up until that time Rangers had missed a mere nine penalties as opposed to the 21 occasions on which Celtic had failed to find the mark. It is easy to see therefore why anyone simply totting up the number of penalty goals could very well be led to an erroneous conclusion.

Any historian will tell you that the byways are always more interesting than the main road and so it is with myths, free from the burden of inconvenient facts. They do no great harm, can easily be disproved and the disproof will have not the slightest hope of checking questions on the same subjects in the years to come.

OLD BLACK BULL (Milngavie) Was there a transfer fee when Billy McPhail moved from Clyde to Celtic? Did he and his brother John play in the same Celtic side?

When Billy McPhail went from Clyde to Celtic on May 5, 1956 there was a transfer fee of £2500. A few days earlier his brother John had quit football after receiving a free transfer from Celtic.

REGAL BAR (Armadale) From which club did Celtic get Ronnie Simpson and who was Hibernian manager at the time?

As I have said several times Jock Stein was manager of Hibernian when Ronnie Simpson left them to play for Celtic in 1964.

MILL'S BAR (Duke Street) I say that Jimmy Delaney has four

cup medals, English, Scottish, Irish and Welsh. My friends say no. Who is right?

Your friends. Jimmy Delaney won a Scottish Cup medal with Aberdeen in 1937, an English one with Manchester United in 1948 and an Irish one with Derry City in 1954. He also had a runners-up medal in the Republic of Ireland but never took part in Welsh football.

J.S. v J.S. (Glasgow) In season 1971-72 did Celtic defeat Rangers three times at Ibrox inside eight days?

No. They won two league cup matches at Ibrox on August 14 and August 28 and then won the league fixture, also at Ibrox, on September 11.

THOMAS FYFE (Glasgow) Will you please confirm that (a) Celtic did not go 50 years without winning at Pittodrie and (b) Jimmy McGrory did score there.

On November 7, 1925 Celtic won 4-2 at Pittodrie with McGrory scoring one of the goals. He also scored there on at least one other occasion. Taking another result almost at random on December 29, 1951 Celtic won 4-3 with two penalties from Collins, an own goal from McKenna and one from Walsh.

CLEARY (Toryglen) I reckon the two penalties awarded by referee Hugh Phillips in a League Cup final is a record for Celtic in Old Firm games

Not quite sure of your drift but if you mean a record for the award of penalties to Celtic the answer is no. In the Glasgow Cup semi-final of season 1941-42 Celtic were awarded three penalties against Rangers at Hampden Park. They missed two of them and ended up losing 3-2.

ROYAL OAK (Nitshill) A man from this area says that about 1929-31 Celtic went through a season losing only one goal with a team including Shaw, McNair and Dodds. Can you verify this?

Don't believe him. The players mentioned are all from an earlier vintage and it did not happen even then.

CHAPTER TEN

High Scores and Scorers

There is a school of thought that says that over the years Celtic have been the Cavaliers of Scottish football to the Roundheads of Rangers. The comparison is imperfect and has not always been true. In the early 1960s for example, Rangers were much the freer-moving and freer-scoring side. But if we mean that for much of their time together Rangers have been the more efficient and Celtic the more daring, there might well be something in it.

Certainly a side which simply won matches without scoring heavily was never likely to endear itself to the support. Victory without swagger, without panache, was not greatly to be prized. The early players who linger in the mind were almost all forwards, Bennett, McMenemy, Quinn, Somers, Hamilton and later Gallagher and McGrory. As for defenders perhaps only Alec McNair and later John Thomson reached such heights of celebrity.

We have mentioned McGrory before but perhaps can be pardoned for coming back to him. A centre-forward or in modern terms a striker who scores once every three games is highly useful. One who scores in every other game he plays in is outstanding. At just over a goal a game McGrory doubled this fine strike rate and he did it not over a handful of matches but in more than 400 league appearances. We can discount the hatfuls of goals against inferior opposition in the Scottish Cup or even the eight against a Dunfermline side out of its depth in the First Division. But there is no gainsaying the five against Aberdeen, the four against St

Just one game's haul! Joe McBride, who was a most prolific goalscorer in his all-too-short spell at Parkhead

Mirren and the three in three minutes against Motherwell.

During the war the inept non-attacking football played by the Celtic side drove thousands away from Parkhead and it is no exaggeration to say that the club did not possess a reputable centre-forward between the departure of Johnny Crum and the arrival for an all too brief period of Billy McPhail in 1956.

A really outstanding league side will score somewhere between 2.5 and 3 goals per match and Celtic exceeded the three per game mark in the first two of their nine championship successes. This may have had something to do with the undoubted fact that defences were less well organised then but much more to do with the fact that Celtic, in McBride, Wallace and Deans, had three leaders tinged with genius. The game was geared to attack, 5-4 at Dunfermline, 5-3 at Easter Road, 5-4 at Dundee.

Nor was it a matter, as nowadays, of keeping the one or at most two danger men quiet. Stop the above mentioned and you still had to deal with the prolific Lennox and Chalmers. Cope with them and Auld and Hughes scored a fair few in their time. When you add to that the incursions of Murdoch from midfield and that Tommy Gemmell reckoned it a poor season in which he did not score 10 goals, then the goal avalanche is easily explained.

European sides did not escape. As good a team as Red Star was on the wrong end of a 5-1 thrashing at Parkhead. Dukla Prague lost three there and three goals were scored at Nantes and Zurich. Domestic opposition was steam-rollered when everybody was on song together, so that even at the semi-final stage of a League Cup Celtic could score seven, and three times against Hibernian at the last stage the Edinburgh side was made to concede six goals. Those in search of the unusual statistic should check out Bobby Lennox's feat of scoring five goals in successive League Cup games in season 1968-69.

The change in the shape of the game in the last twenty years has meant that increasingly goals must be shared around, with midfield players becoming major contributors. This is not a plus for spectators. Much more thrilling to see Joe McBride score 37 by December than to see three midfielders score a dozen each and in recent years the midfield well has dried up badly with the loss of such as Murdo MacLeod and Billy Stark.

Under Stein in particular Celtic brought off the difficult mix of elegance and ruthlessness and although in the short term a success is needed no matter how achieved, the support will not be happy until a three or four goal victory can be accepted calmly as nothing out of the way. Until that day comes again the exploits of such as McGrory, McBride, Lennox, Chalmers and Wallace must serve as beacons for the future.

HIGH SCORES AND HIGH SCORERS

TINY (Maryhill) Did Celtic ever figure in a game where they led 4-0 after 20 minutes and it ended in a 4-4 draw?

What happened was even more remarkable. In a league game against Third Lanark at Parkhead in September 1963 Celtic led 4-0 after 16 minutes, Divers, Lennox, Turner and Brogan being their scorers. Anderson (2), and Buckley brought the score back to 4-3 by half-time and Graham equalised, in the 49th minute.

J. S. (Bothwell) After Celtic won the Scottish Cup in 1937 beating Aberdeen 2-1 they were beaten 8-0 in a league game at Motherwell. Am I correct in saying that the Motherwell centre-forward, Stewart, had six goals that night?

He scored six on April 30, 1937 and the other Motherwell scorers were Ogilvie and Stevenson.

J. R. (Leverndale, Crookston) Did Jimmy McGrory score eight goals for Celtic in one match?

He had eight goals for Celtic when they beat Dunfermline Athletic 9-0 in a league game at Parkhead in January 1928.

J. E (Alva) Can you supply both teams and the score in the Celtic v Airdrie game when Frank Haffey missed a penalty kick?

At Parkhead on October 26, 1963 when Celtic won 9-0 the teams were, CELTIC, Haffey, Young, Gemmell, Clark, McNeill, Kennedy, Gallagher, Murdoch, Chalmers, Divers, Hughes.

One of many – Bobby Lennox opens the scoring against St Johnstone in a league match at Parkhead in October 1968

AIRDRIE, McKenzie, Black, Keenan, Rowan, Hannah, Johnstone, McColl, Murray, Boyd, Reid, Jeffrey.

Roddy McKenzie made a fine save from Frank Haffey's penalty.

BURNBANK (Glasgow) Have you any record of Jimmy McGrory scoring four goals against St Mirren in a competitive match?

In a league match at Parkhead in January 1922 the Celtic centre-forward scored four in a 6-2 win for Celtic.

WEE MAC (Dumbarton) Has a visiting player ever scored four goals in a competitive match at Easter Road?

There may well be other instances but Joe McBride certainly did this as a Celtic player when his side won 5-3 at Easter Road in October 1966.

BIG INVER (Barlanark) I remember John Hughes scoring five goals against Aberdeen while wearing sandshoes. Can you give me further details?

This was a league game played at Parkhead on January 30, 1965 when Celtic won 8-0. Their other scorers were Lennox, Murdoch and Auld, pen.

CORMACK (Partick) Did Jimmy McGrory ever score five goals with headers in a league match against Aberdeen?

No, but in October 1926 he scored five against the Dons, all but one of which were headers.

AULD LANG SYNE (Glasgow) Details please of the 1972 Scottish Cup Final between Celtic and Hibernian.

Celtic won this match 6-1 and the teams were, CELTIC, Williams, Craig, Brogan, Murdoch, McNeill, Connelly, Johnstone, Deans, Macari, Dalglish, Callaghan.

HIBERNIAN, Herriot, Brownlie, Schaedler, Stanton, Black, Blackley, Edwards, Hazel, Gordon, O'Rourke, Duncan.

Scorers for Celtic were Deans (3), McNeill, Macari (2), and for Hibernian Gordon scored.

GEORGE THOMSON (Glasgow) Was Jimmy Quinn the first player to score a hat-trick in a Scottish Cup Final?

Yes, he netted all three against Rangers in the Scottish Cup Final of 1904. Dixie Deans is the other Celtic player to have accomplished this feat, against Hibernian in 1972.

RIGHT HALF BAR (Glasgow) Please give the highest scores over the last 20 years (1956-76) in the Scottish Cup, League Cup and Glasgow Cup finals and the teams involved on each occasion.

As I suspect you know, Celtic hold each of these records, beating Hibernian 6-1 in the 1972 Scottish Cup Final, Rangers 7-1 in the League Cup Final of 1957 and Clyde 8-0 in the Glasgow Cup Final of 1967-68.

CAMPBELL PARKER (Saltcoats) How many goals did Bobby Lennox score in domestic cup-ties in season 1966-67?

I make it that he scored 5 League Cup goals, 5 Scottish Cup goals and 7 Glasgow Cup goals, netting in all 17 times.

ON THE BALL (Lanark) Can you remember a day in the 1960s when between them the Old Firm scored 15 goals in the league on the same day?

This certainly happened on December 16, 1967 when Rangers hammered Raith Rovers 10-2 at Ibrox. The same day Celtic beat Dundee 5-4 at Dens Park.

CHAPTER ELEVEN

Celtic in Wartime Football

There could hardly be a greater contrast than that between Celtic's records in the First and Second World Wars. Between 1914-19 Celtic won the Scottish League on four occasions out of a possible five, (the official league continued although somewhat illogically the Scottish Cup was suspended for the duration of the war.) During this time the club went a record 63 league matches undefeated and performed such feats as winning two league matches in a single day.

Even now questions come in about the great sides of 1911-20. There is absolutely no doubt that during this period Celtic were the pre-eminent team in Scotland.

The Second World War experience was vastly different. War came in the season after the great Celtic side of 1938 had won the Exhibition Cup and the League in 1937-38 in the club's Golden Jubilee Year. Right from the outbreak of war in September 1939 it seemed as if Celtic had no real interest in war-time football, to such an extent that one could seriously question why they bothered to take part in it at all.

This lack of commitment showed itself in various ways, one of which was the reluctance to employ guest players after the first two wartime seasons. This policy achieved a splendid perversity when such a player as Matt Busby had the offer of his services refused. He went off to Easter Road to bring on such young Hibernian starlets as Bobby Combe and Gordon Smith. Nor was he the only player to have his offer declined with thanks. The O'Donnell brothers, Frank and Hugh, who had returned to Scotland were likewise informed that their former club was not interested. Nor could Willie Buchan nor Charlie Napier persuade the Parkhead chiefs to give them a game.

This was perhaps because Celtic would not depart from the strict wartime ruling of £2 per game per player. This was either laudably law-abiding or betokened a certain miserliness at a time when the rule was being flaunted. Certainly we have to ask ourselves why Napier and Buchan both found it worthwhile to play with Stenhousemuir in that first wartime season of 1939-1940.

There was no earthly reason why Celtic should not have run a reserve side during the war as Rangers did from 1941, but the decision was taken not to do so. As a result, as the war progressed, the Celtic side came to consist increasingly of optimistic signings from the juveniles and Boys Guild teams. Over the whole six years of the war the trophy haul was one miserable success apiece in the Glasgow Cup and the Glasgow Charity Cup. Absolutely no impact was made in the wartime Southern League or Southern League Cup. This was combined with some spectacularly heavy defeats, four goals being lost to Dumbarton at Parkhead, six to Falkirk at Brockville and most damagingly of all, eight to Rangers in the painful New Year's Day game of 1943.

Celtic could not fairly claim that it was loss of front-line players to the forces that brought about this predicament. Of the 1938 side Joe Kennaway, the goalkeeper, went back to the United States and Canada while Willie Lyon and George Paterson joined the army and the air force respectively. Every other member of the side was available throughout the war but by 1945 only Hogg, MacDonald and Delaney were turning out for Celtic.

Reluctance to pay came to a head in 1943 when three Celtic players, Johnny Crum, Johnny Divers and Johnny Kelly turned out in a Southern League match for Morton against Celtic. The club's attitude was a great let-down to their thousands of supporters in the Forces who had to suffer the taunts of their Old Firm rivals as Celtic's performances became a matter of ridicule.

The policy was also grossly unfair to the then manager Jimmy McStay who had to try to manage for a Board of Directors which conveyed the impression that it was sublimely uninterested in what was going on.

Had this just been a matter of missing out on unofficial wartime trophies then perhaps it might not have mattered so much. But when peace came again in 1945 Celtic were appallingly unprepared for it. Good players such as Delaney and Paterson had tagged the club as unambitious and were off. For the first six years after the war the team was nondescript, middle-of-the league, bundled out of the Scottish Cup at an early stage. Yet the odd great player did emerge, Willie Miller in goal for one, Bobby Evans at right-half though initially an inside-forward, for another.

These are the players who still draw the questions. Interestingly, as the Celtic team performance has slumped in the late 1980s and early 1990s there has been a revival of interest in wartime performance, as though to re-assure the questioners that things could never be quite as bad as they were from 1939-50. In sport one must learn from opponents and there was much to admire in the manner in which Bill Struth of Rangers had thought. "Well, there is wartime football, if we participate we have to be whole-hearted about it. For my own part that means seeing to the availability of my players and by running a reserve side giving as many of them as possible a game." At the other end of the city Jimmy McStay would have given much for such backing.

WAR TIME FOOTBALL

OLD FIRM PALS (Nitshill) Please oblige with the Celtic team that beat Third Lanark in the Glasgow Charity Cup final of 1943.

The following side won 3-0. Miller, Hogg, Dornan, Corbett, McLaughlin, Paterson, Delaney, McPhail, Rae, McGinley, Long.

S.L.W. (Glasgow) Can you recall a Glasgow Cup final during the Second World War when Celtic were leading Rangers 2-0

but lost. **Was Willie Corbett injured? Please give teams, scorers, venue and say who became Celtic's centre-half if Corbett was out through injury.**

This was the Glasgow Cup final of 1944 in which Corbett was injured. The match was played at Hampden Park and the teams were, CELTIC, Miller, P McDonald, McAulay, M MacDonald, Corbett, Paterson, Lynch, Evans, McKay, McPhail, McLaughlin. RANGERS, Jenkins, Gray, Shaw, Watkins, Young, Symon, McKinnon, Gillick, Waddell, Duncanson, Johnston.

Scorers for Rangers were Waddell, Symon, Young, pen and for Celtic Lynch and McKay. Jimmy Mallan filled the centre-half berth for the rest of that season.

M.S. (Cranhill) If Celtic Park was closed at any time during the last war can you give the reason and did Celtic play any home games at Shawfield during the closure?

After a disturbance at a Rangers v Celtic game at Ibrox the SFA closed Celtic Park from September 18 to October 17, 1941. In that time Celtic had away matches with Hamilton Academical, Morton, Hibernian and St Mirren and one 'home' game with Motherwell at Shawfield on October 4.

ALWAYS GREEN (Balloch) Did Dumbarton beat Celtic 4-1 at Parkhead in a wartime game?

On September 4, 1943 in a Southern League match Dumbarton recorded such a win. Gallacher scored for Celtic and Lipton (2), Hepburn and Reid were the Dumbarton scorers.

HOPEFUL (Gallowgate) Was Frank Murphy of Celtic ordered off against Albion Rovers in a wartime match?

He was sent off in a wartime game at Cliftonhill in 1941.

D. LAPPIN (Glasgow) Please tell me when during the war John McPhail played his first game for Celtic.

John tells me his first game for Celtic was in mid-October 1941 in a Southern League match against Partick Thistle at Parkhead.

POSSIL BAR (Glasgow) Did Celtic play guest players during the war years?

In the early years of the war, 1940 and 1941 they had quite a few guest players of whom Gillan of Alloa, Hunter of

Kilmarnock, Waddell and Johnstone of Aberdeen were the most notable. From about 1942 they tended to concentrate on home-produced players which was spectacularly unsuccessful.

PAUL LUNNEY (Possilpark) Did Celtic win any trophies while Jimmy McStay was manager during the Second World War?

Jimmy McStay had only two successes and these were the Glasgow Cup of 1940 when Rangers were beaten 1-0 and the Charity Cup of 1943 when Third Lanark were beaten 3-0.

R.A.M.N. (Anderston) How many Old Firm players were in the Forces during the last war?

If we are talking about those who were first team players in 1939 the answer is very few. Of the Rangers side Willie Thornton, Davie Kinnear and Tom McKillop, who could be considered a fringe player, were all in the armed forces and of the Celtic Exhibition Cup winning side only Willie Lyon and George Paterson saw armed service.

CHAPTER TWELVE

Oddities – Love of the Quirky

When a football club is more than 100 years old it is odds-on that many strange things will have happened to it in that time and many questions to me lie in this area. Prominent personalities who have watched Old Firm matches include film star Danny Kaye and Prime Minister Harold McMillan. Supporters are keen to link improbable trebles and quadruples, the equivalent of the roll-up bet presumably, and from time to time the question comes, "Did Celtic ever have a Canadian, a Swedish and a Jewish goalkeeper?" It is an imaginative question and a pity that the answer is no, the name Joe Coen, who played for a while in the early 1930s, misleading some supporters.

The man who played in bare feet actually did not do so since he played with tightly bound bandages. But who would have thought that an Indian seaman who played only two reserve matches almost 60 years ago should still be in people's minds.

There is also a fixation with the penalty spot. Did a Celtic player ever score three penalties in a competitive match. He did. Did Celtic ever miss three penalty kicks in a competitive match? They did. Have Celtic been awarded three penalty kicks in the same match on more than one occasion? They have. Sometimes it seems that no matter how improbable the question, the answer is always yes.

Most people who saw the highly-individual Tommy McInally in the 20s do not exactly recall him as a greyhound, but he nevertheless did beat one of the great sprinters of his time in a 100 yards sprint, although he was receiving a fair handicap

There is a wish, gratified, to be told that Alan Morton and Patsy Gallagher played in the same side. When it comes to unusual ways of losing points there is the game against Queen's Park when the referee blew for time two minutes early with Celtic in the lead and on the re-emergence from the pavilion the Amateurs salvaged the match.

There are the interesting personal face-offs such as that which saw Bobby Lennox's opponent in his first match for Celtic being Craig Brown of Dundee, the present Scotland manager. The fiasco of the flag on the enclosure comes up often and some supporters are surprised to learn that Celtic's stoutest supporters in this fracas with the SFA were Rangers, until they sit down and think it through.

What else? Well, the Celtic player who scored on his Scotland debut without kicking a ball is clearly worthy of a mention as is the referee who tossed up in a Scottish Cup final with a 50p piece two years before the introduction of decimal coinage.

The win in orange stockings in a European Cup tie appears to give particular satisfaction to a vocal minority and what Sherlock Holmes might have called the Case of the Brazilian Trialists continues to occupy minds.

People remember George Connelly's exhibition of ball-juggling before a European match but forget which one for the moment. And have Celtic goalkeepers ever worn red jerseys? And what was the match when Denis Connaghan threw the ball into his own goal? And did Celtic once lose three goals to a works team in the Scottish Cup? When I tell you that they did and as recently as 1939 at that, you will understand that the unusual, the strange, what the poet Burns would have called the unco', is liable to continue to form a substantial proportion of questions asked.

ODDITIES

NEUTRAL (Newarthill) Have you the date and teams involved when the American cinema star Danny Kaye attended a Cup final at Hampden?

Danny Kaye saw Celtic beat Rangers 3-2 in the final of the Glasgow Charity Cup at Hampden in May 1950.

OLD TIMER (Baillieston) Concerning Dr William Kivlichan who played for both Celtic and Rangers, can you tell me if he ever played for Celtic in a Scottish Cup final?

The Celtic team which beat Hamilton Academicals 2-0 after a 0-0 draw at Ibrox in 1911 was, Adams, McNair, Hay, Young, McAteer, Dodds, McAtee, McMenemy, Quinn, Kivlichan, Hamilton.

BILLY Q. (Lennoxtown) Has a Celtic player ever scored three penalties in a competitive match?

Bobby Collins had all three Celtic goals from the spot in a 3-0 win over Aberdeen in a league match at Parkhead on September 26, 1953.

DAPP (Drumchapel) Did Giles Heron or any other player ever play barefooted for Celtic?

Abdul Salim, an Indian seaman from a ship docked in Glasgow, played at outside-right for two reserve matches in season 1935-36 and instead of wearing boots played with bandaged feet. This is probably what you have in mind. Giles Heron from Detroit wore normal boots in all his games for Celtic.

ANOTHER ADMIRER (Scotstoun) Regarding Celtic recently (1971) buying one of Charlie Tully's medals, can you confirm that during the Second World War, Jimmy McMenemy gave some of the medals won as a Celtic player to one of the Glasgow War Funds?

In July 1940 Jimmy McMenemy handed over four gold medals (Scottish Cup 1911, Charity Cup 1917, and two trainer's medals) to Lord Provost Patrick Dollan. They were sold to an East End admirer of McMenemy for £50 which went to the Lord Provost's Relief Fund.

GERRY REYNOLDS (Glasgow) During what match did George Connelly of Celtic do his famous "keepy-uppy" exhibition? I say it was during a European match at Parkhead.

George Connelly states that it was during the European Cup Winners Cup match against Dynamo Kiev at Parkhead on January 12, 1966.

CALLING WATTIE (Hamilton)

I am sure the occasion you have in mind is when Celtic defeated Raith Rovers 6-0 at Parkhead on the afternoon of Saturday April 15, 1916 and on the same evening defeated Motherwell 3-1 at Fir Park.

GET SET (Oatlands) Have you any record of Tommy McInally beating the great sprinter W R Applegarth in a sprint at a sports meeting?

On October 5, 1920 McInally beat Applegarth over 100 yards at Shawfield. Applegarth was giving away 10 yards to his opponent and finished third.

E. T. (Glasgow) I maintain that in the early years of this century Willie Kivlichan signed for Rangers and later moved to Celtic.

Willie Kivlichan had one full season with Rangers, appearing in 11 league matches before moving to Parkhead in May 1907.

BOUNDARY BAR (Springburn) Did Alec Bennet of the great Celtic forward line of Bennet, McMenemy, Quinn, Somers and Hamilton ever play for Rangers and if so in what position?

Alec Bennet had 3 or 4 years at Ibrox immediately before World War One and he played on both wings.

HOLY WILLIE (Paisley) When was Celtic's first Sunday match and who did they play?

Their first Sunday match was a Scottish Cup tie at Parkhead against Clydebank in season 1973-74 which they won 6-1.

JACK THE LAD (Paisley) Did Alan Morton and Patsy Gallagher ever play in the same side?

Yes, in friendlies and for Glasgow. One such occasion was the Glasgow v Sheffield match at Hampden in 1924.

WEE JOHN (Carmyle) How many goals did Bobby Lennox

score to win the **Golden Boot Bronze** award in 1968?

Lennox scored 32 goals to finish ten behind Eusebio of Benfica who won the gold. The Hungarian Dumai of Ujpest Dosza was second with 36 goals.

THE LONG BAR (Hamilton.) When Bobby Lennox played his first game for Celtic who was his direct opponent? Did Lennox have his nose broken accidentally during this game?

I saw this match and I do not remember the player sustaining a facial injury. Interestingly his direct opponent that day was the present Scotland manager, Craig Brown.

GARVEL VIEW (Craigend) Back in 1930 in a league game Celtic led Queen's Park when the referee blew for time two minutes early. Am I right in saying that the teams came out again and the Amateurs equalised ? Please give teams and scorers.

The incident was as you describe it with Celtic leading 3-2 at the first final whistle. Will have the teams for you soon but meanwhile I can tell you that the scorers were McLelland, Crawford and McAlpine for Queen's Park while Charlie Napier (2), and Bertie Thomson netted for Celtic.

YER OULD DA (Linwood) In a game between East Fife and Celtic at Methil in 1973 Celtic missed three penalties, one of them a retake. Who were the players who missed?

Murdoch missed the first, the referee ordered a retake and Hood missed. Dalglish had another penalty saved by the East Fife keeper Ernie McGarr. The match was played in February 1973.

LISBON LION (Springburn) Did Celtic remove the Irish flag from the top of the enclosure when ordered to do so by the SFA?

In 1952 Celtic were ordered to remove the flag but after taking legal opinion refused to do so. The SFA then dropped the matter.

BURNHEAD BOWLING CLUB (Stenhousemuir) Please give all relevant details of the Scottish Cup tie at Brockville when Charlie Tully scored with two successive corner kicks, the first of which was disallowed.

Celtic won this 3-2 on February 21, 1953. Teams were,

FALKIRK, McFeat, McDonald, Rae, Gallacher, McKenzie, Hunter, Delaney, Dunlop, Weir, Campbell, Brown.

CELTIC, Bonnar, Haughney, Meechan, Evans, Stein, McPhail, Collins, Walsh, McGrory, Fernie, Tully.

Scorers were Weir and Campbell for Falkirk and Tully, Fernie and McGrory for Celtic.

G.G. (Glasgow) When Bobby Lennox broke an ankle against Rangers at Ibrox what was the original decision and who was the referee?

Mr E Thomson of Edinburgh awarded a penalty for the tackle on Lennox by John Greig but after consulting a linesman awarded a free-kick for offside against another Celtic forward. I saw the game and think that this was a correct decision.

E. CAMERON (Uddingston) Who was the Scottish international who only played one match for his country and scored a goal without kicking a ball?

This was Joe Craig of Celtic who came on as a sub against Sweden at Hampden on April 27, 1977 and scored with his first touch, a header in a 3-1 win.

CALLING CLYDESDALE WORKS (Bellshill)

I can confirm that a 50p piece was used to toss up in the 1969 Scottish Cup Final between Celtic and Rangers. Mr Jim Callaghan Jr writes to say that his father, the match referee, was among the first to be given one of the new coins and it may have been used on Cup Final day as a publicity stunt. He had originally intended to use a coin donated by the New Zealand FA.

W. SMITH (Craigend) In the early 1960s Celtic had two Brazilian trialists on their books. Who signed them and how long were they there?

Jock Stein had just taken over as manager at Parkhead when four Brazilian trialists arrived in 1965. Ayrton Inacio and Marco di Sousa played for the reserves while Jorge Farah and Fernando Consul appeared only in practice matches. They were at Parkhead for a few months only although subsequently Inacio turned out for Clydebank.

OFF TARGET (Bridgeton) Did Willie McStay ever miss three penalties in the one match against Falkirk?

Can't trace this but in a match against Falkirk at Parkhead on December 9, 1922 he missed two and scored with the third. The match ended in a 1-1 draw with the Falkirk goal, scored by Scott, also coming from the penalty spot.

CHAPTER THIRTEEN

The One-Off Cups

Throughout their hundred years and more of history Celtic have shown a tremendous talent for winning the one-off competition. This facility goes back to the time of the Ibrox Disaster of 1902 when they won the Glasgow Exhibition Cup which Rangers had acquired the previous year. Rangers, Sunderland and Everton were the teams to take part.

Celtic did not win the Victory Cup of 1919 any more than they did that of 1946 (a fertile source of letters this last one), but this is eclipsed by the winning of the biggest Anglo-Scottish competition of all time, the Empire Exhibition tournament of 1938, run at Ibrox in conjunction with the great show in the Bellahouston Park. The Old Firm, Hearts and Aberdeen represented Scotland with Sunderland, Everton, Chelsea and Brentford who were then a power in the land, making up the English entry. On their way to the trophy Celtic disposed of Sunderland, after two games, then narrowly beat a splendid Hearts side before going to extra time to beat Everton and take the cup.

For any Celtic supporter over fifty the Exhibition team trips off the tongue almost more easily than the Lisbon Lions. The heroes of 1938 were Kennaway, Hogg, Morrison, Geatons, Lyon, Paterson, Delaney, MacDonald, Crum, Divers, Murphy. This was the last great pre-war flourish of that notable Celtic team.

Came the end of the war and a victory on corners in the VE

Cup over a strong Queen's Park side which could consider itself unlucky.

Not as unlucky as Celtic in the Victory Cup semi-final of 1946 when in the replay outrageously incompetent refereeing by M C Dale led to a 2-0 defeat and suspensions for three players, one of whom, Matt Lynch, had neither been sent off nor officially cautioned. Readers often write to ask if Jimmy Duncanson of Rangers wrote a letter of support for Matt Lynch to submit to the SFA. The answer is that he did, I have seen the letter, and the SFA took absolutely no notice of it.

Five years later Celtic were back at Hampden and winning the Festival of Britain Trophy, giving Aberdeen two goals of a start in doing so. This led to the famous situation in which the trophy, proudly accepted by the winners, turned out to be an old bowling trophy in a perilous state of disrepair.

One could argue that when Celtic won the Empire Exhibition Cup in 1938 it was scarcely a surprise. They had after all won the league in the same season. When it was decided to mark the Coronation of Queen Elizabeth in 1953 with a similar tournament, Celtic hardly made a case for inclusion, except on gate-drawing and sentimental grounds. They had slipped from the ranks of the leading Scottish clubs and were making no sort of league challenge. Nevertheless with Rangers, Hibernian and Aberdeen they defended the national honour against Arsenal, Manchester United, Newcastle United and Tottenham Hotspur.

Once again the challenge was good for Celtic. They put out Arsenal and then did the same for Manchester United, fresh from defeating Rangers. In the final there were more than 117,000 at Hampden to see the Celtic goalkeeper John Bonnar play the game of his career to withstand the sublimely gifted Hibernian forward line of Smith, Johnstone, Reilly, Turnbull, Ormond and allow his colleagues to steal upfield and register two spectacular breakaway goals from Neil Mochan and Jimmy Walsh.

There were various other one-off cups won on foreign tour and in invitation matches at Parkhead but the really big one, the unofficial World Championship against Racing Club from

Argentina got away. It need not have done with firmer refereeing or better preparation from the Parkhead end and it need not have been lost at all had not Sir Robert Kelly most uncharacteristically allowed himself to be persuaded to carry out the third match in Montevideo when all his instincts warned him not to.

These were great matches, even the shambles in Montevideo had a certain grim epic grandeur about it.

And the questions? Who was the Celtic player ordered off in Montevideo who did not leave the field? Answer, Bertie Auld. It figures!

In the Coronation Cup my readers all wish to remind me that Joe Mercer of Arsenal had played for Everton in the Empire Exhibition Trophy of 1938. Strangely they almost always omit an even stranger detail, namely that George Hamilton played for the same club, Aberdeen, in both competitions. Much more remarkable.

Some correspondents argue that clubs develop characteristics as humans do, almost to the extent of acquiring a corporate personality. There may well be something in this. Certainly the dash and risk-taking of Cup football have always seemed to appeal to Celtic. In tight situations Tully scored direct from two corner kicks in immediate succession (only one counted), and in the Festival of Britain tournament he quick-thinkingly threw the ball against the back of an Aberdeen defender, won a corner and a goal resulted which put Celtic back in the hunt.

For long stretches of Old Firm history it has been tempting to think in racing terms of Celtic the sprinter against Rangers the stayer. Not always, of course. There was league domination and to spare in the Stein era, but often Rangers have been the better bet for the long road. Should a one-off tournament be organised in the season to come, history, and the smart money might be on Celtic.

CELTIC IN ONE OFF CUPS

J. D. (Yoker) Can you oblige with the Celtic and Hibernian sides in the Coronation Cup Final of 1953? In how many of these matches was John McPhail at left-half?

Teams at Hampden on May 20, 1953 when Celtic won 2-0 were, CELTIC, Bonnar, Haughney, Rollo, Evans, Stein, McPhail, Collins, Walsh, Mochan, Peacock, Fernie.

HIBERNIAN, Younger, Govan, Paterson, Buchanan, Howie, Combe, Smith, Johnstone, Reilly, Turnbull, Ormond.

John McPhail was at left-half for all three games of the competition.

CUMBRAE (Dennistoun) A few weeks ago in reply to Wee Pub (Easterhouse) you were not sure about Celtic and Clyde playing a 4-4 draw at Firhill. This game was in the second round of the St Mungo Cup, played before the start of the 1951-52 season. Celtic won the replay 4-1 which was also at Firhill.

Thanks for the reminder. This tournament was held to celebrate the Festival of Britain in 1951. The drawn game was at Firhill on a Thursday evening and the replay took place on the following night.

LISBON TIM (Glasgow) Did Neil Mochan win two cup medals with Celtic before he played a home match for them?

He has this unusual distinction. He was signed in May 1953 and made his first appearance against Queen's Park in the Glasgow Charity Cup final when Celtic won 3-1. Within a fortnight he had a Coronation Cup medal – and all before Mochan ran out at Parkhead in a Celtic strip.

GEORGE McCANN (Glasgow) I maintain that Jimmy Delaney played for Aberdeen against Celtic in the St Mungo Cup final of 1951.

Quickest way to prove that he did not is to give you the Aberdeen forward line on that night which was Bogan, Yorston, Hamilton, Baird, Hather.

CELTIC FAN (Cranhill) Please give the Celtic side which beat Aberdeen in the final of the St Mungo Cup.

Celtic won this trophy on August 1, 1951 when they beat Aberdeen 3-2, having been 2-0 down. Team read, Hunter, Haughney, Rollo, Evans, Mallan, Baillie, Collins, Walsh, Fallon, Peacock, Tully.

B.L. (U. S. A.) Who were the Celtic players sent off in the World Club Cup Championship match in South America?

In the match in Montevideo on November 4, 1967 Bobby Lennox, Jimmy Johnstone and John Hughes were sent off. In the referee's report reference was made to Bertie Auld also having been dismissed but he did not leave the field at any time.

NINE IN A ROW (Garngad) When Celtic played and beat Real Madrid in a friendly in Spain how long was it after the European Cup Final?

Celtic beat Real Madrid 1-0 at the Bernabeu Stadium two weeks after their triumph in Lisbon against Inter Milan.

SPUD (Glasgow)When Charlie Tully threw the ball against David Shaw of Aberdeen in the St Mungo Cup final was he booked and who was the referee?

Jack Mowat was the official in charge of this match which Celtic won 3-2. Tully was not booked. He took the corner which was awarded and from it Sean Fallon scored Celtic's first goal.

As to your other question the scorers in this match were Fallon (2), and Walsh for Celtic, and Yorston and Bogan for Aberdeen.

SADIE (Govan) Please give the Celtic side which beat Queen's Park in the V E Trophy played in May 1945.

On May 9, 1945 Celtic and Queen's Park drew 1-1 at Hampden, Celtic taking the cup on corner kicks. Their team was, Miller, Hogg, P McDonald, Lynch, Mallan, McPhail, Paton, M McDonald, Gallacher, Evans, McLaughlin.

WHISTLING SANDY (Burnbank) Please give the Scottish and English clubs which took part in the Coronation Cup of 1953.

The Scottish sides were Aberdeen, Celtic, Hibernian and Rangers and their English counterparts were Arsenal, Manchester United, Newcastle United and Tottenham Hotspur.

WEE TAM (Glasgow) I say that when Celtic took part in the Coronation Cup in 1953 they were not qualified to do so either as Scottish Cup winners or as first or second in the league.

You are correct. Celtic were probably included on gate potential and memories of their performance in the Empire Exhibition Cup of 1938.

JOHN BAXTER (Glasgow) Recently you mentioned Rangers, Hearts and Motherwell as prominent Scottish sides which had played in the Anglo-Scottish Cup. Did Celtic ever play in this competition?

In season 1978-79 Celtic lost 1-0 to Burnley at Turf Moor and 2-1 at Parkhead.

DANCING JACK (Glasgow) Can you give scores and crowds in Celtic's three matches in the Coronation Cup of 1953?

In winning this Celtic beat Arsenal 1-0, attendance 60,000; Manchester United 2-1, attendance 73,000; and Hibernian 2-0, attendance 108,000.

R.S. (Glasgow) How many Celtic players took part in the Empire Exhibition tournament of 1938?

Thirteen. In addition to the winning side of Kennaway, Hogg, Morrison, Geatons, Lyon, Paterson, Delaney, McDonald, Crum, Divers, Murphy two other players, Matt Lynch and Joe Carruth, also took part.

PHIL'S MATE (Barrachnie) Please give details of a mid-week cup final when Celtic lost 4-1 to Rangers and had two men sent off.

A touch of confusion here. The only game that fits is the replayed semi-final of the Victory Cup in 1946 when Rangers won 2-0. Teams then were, RANGERS, Brown, Cox, Shaw, Watkins, Young, Symon, Waddell, Gillick, Thornton, Duncanson, Caskie. CELTIC, Miller, Hogg, Mallan, Lynch, Corbett, McAuley, Sirrell, Kiernan, Gallacher, Paterson, Paton.

Scorers for Rangers were Thornton and Young (pen.). Mallan and Paterson were sent off and later Lynch was suspended although he was not cautioned during the game and Jimmy Duncanson of Rangers wrote in his defence.

DOUBLE D (Glasgow) Please give the Celtic team and scorers for the second-leg game against Sedan in the Friendship Cup.

This match, played at Parkhead on October 18, 1960 saw the following side get a 3-3 draw, Haffey, McKay, Kennedy, Crerand, McNeill, Peacock, Chalmers, Fernie, Carroll, Divers, Auld. Scorers were Divers and Chalmers (2).

DIAMOND JIM (Glasgow) I have a medal which says Celtic FC, Cologne 31. 5. 22 and on the other side "British Forces on the Rhine." Can you tell me anything about it?

There is no trace of Celtic having played in Cologne on that date but two days previously they drew 1-1 with a German Select in Berlin on the ground which should have hosted the Olympic Games in 1916. If there was some kind of friendly in Cologne the papers of the time did not think it worth reporting.

CALAMITY JANE (King's Park) When Celtic played Racing Club at Hampden in the first leg of the World Club Championship of 1967 how many players were in the Celtic side who had not played in Lisbon?

John Hughes for Steve Chalmers represented the only change from the Lisbon Lions eleven.

NON COMPETITIVE GAMES AGAINST FOREIGN OPPOSITION

TOM K. (Glasgow) What was the charge for the terracing when Celtic met Real Madrid in a friendly at Parkhead?

This match could be seen on the terracing for six shillings (30 pence) on September 10, 1962.

ROYAL BAR (Larkhall) Can you give Celtic's goal times in all three World Club Championship games in South America?

Only two of these games were actually played in South America. At Hampden McNeill scored in 70 minutes to give Celtic a 1-0 win. At Buenos Aires a Gemmell penalty in 22 minutes could not stave off a 2-1 defeat and in the decider at Montevideo in Uruguay, Racing Club won 1-0. These matches were not officially recognised by FIFA.

SARACEN (Lambhill) When did Celtic play Penarol and what was the score? Were Penarol world club champions at the time?

This match was played at Parkhead on September 5, 1967 and Celtic won 2-1. Penarol were world club champions at the time but of course the title was unofficial. Willie Wallace scored both Celtic goals.

CHAPTER FOURTEEN

Internationalists and Internationals

It is a long time since major internationals were played at Parkhead but as long as questions are asked about the Rosebery strip and the hat-trick of R S McColl, so long will these early matches stay in the memory. Since that day in 1900 many a Celt has gone on to give distinguished service to his country, although that country was not always Scotland.

First of all, let us deal with the grievance that Celtic players have continuously been overlooked by their country and barracked unmercifully when they have been chosen by those whose allegiance is to other clubs. There is something in this.

It is astonishing that Jimmy McGrory did not play at Wembley. Bob McPhail certainly thought so. It is a matter of wonder too that Lennox, himself under-used by Scotland, was the first Celtic player to score at Wembley and that was as late as 1967. To this must be added the fact that at different times Celtic players such as Bobby Evans and Jimmy Johnstone asked to be left out of consideration for the national side. There are those who think that Bobby Hogg, Willie Miller and Jimmy Delaney should also have figured more frequently.

We have to ask ourselves two questions. What was the competition these Celts faced and was the club singled out for this treatment? Willie Miller played very few full internationals for Scotland but so too did Bobby Brown of Rangers, a highly-accomplished goalkeeper. Bobby Hogg was a splendid club full back, so too was Dougie Gray of Rangers and throughout their careers they had to yield place to Andy Anderson of Hearts and Jimmy Carabine of Third Lanark. When letters arrive complaining of the treatment afforded Jimmy Delaney it is well to mutter the names of Gordon Smith and Willie Waddell, both in contention for the right wing spot and remember that Jimmy Delaney's arm injuries caused genuine insurance problems.

It should be remembered too that the team was picked in those days by the Selection Committee which meant that almost every side picked was guaranteed one bizarre selection to justify the Selectors "jaunts to England" in the course of the season.

When we work out that probably the greatest inside trio in Scottish football since 1939, namely Conn, Bauld and Wardhaugh of Hearts had exactly six caps among them, then perhaps things fall into place and much can be attributed simply to the failure of the Selectors to recognise class.

Before 1914 Alec McNair and Jimmy Quinn took the honours. People are surprised that so far back, McNair's international career spanned fourteen years. Between the wars McGrory and McPhail of Rangers turned over England often enough at Hampden Park to make Scots wish they had been allowed to try at Wembley. It was at Wembley that Johnny Crum, not the most likely of Celtic caps at that time in his career (1936) and appearing on the right wing was tripped in the box, so allowing Tommy Walker to score his famous penalty equaliser. Had he lived John Thomson would have made the goalkeeping spot his own. In the agreeable custom of the time those who were good club players but not much more, were picked against the Continental sides and thus Frank Murphy played against Holland and could sign himself ever afterwards as "Celtic and Scotland."

Not a few writers of letters to me have picked up on the strange fact that a quite undistinguished Celtic side after 1945 supplied more players to the national side on a regular basis than the much better teams in the 1930s had done. The tireless Bobby Evans,

Bobby Collins who proved that a football brain could offset lack of inches, and Willie Fernie, capped in five positions and perhaps a victim of his own versatility, all featured prominently when the teams were announced. A little later, just before the arrival of Jock Stein, Pat Crerand was as automatic a pick at right-half as Jim Baxter was at left-half. And shortly after that a young centre-half, McNeill came through who looked every bit as appropriate a national captain as he had done at club level.

With the Stein years Celtic players were selected – on at least one occasion there were six of them in a Scotland side. Ronnie Simpson started off in international life at 37 – now there was a man who had cause for grievance when he saw what had been picked ahead of him when he was at Newcastle. As was inevitable in that great year of his he started at the top with a win at Wembley against the then World Cup holders.

Questions, questions. "Which two Lions were ordered off in international matches?" Answer, Bertie Auld and Tommy Gemmell.

"Did Jimmy Johnstone and Willie Henderson ever play in the same international team?" Answer yes.

"Did Jimmy Delaney ever score the winner in an international match against England? Describe it if so." The last sentence is a dead give-away and means the enquirer was there but the answer must be given. Victory International of 1946 at Hampden which Scotland won 1-0 with a last-minute Delaney goal which came as follows. Free kick to Scotland 40 yards out on the left touchline, taken by Jackie Husband of Thistle, Scotland attacking the Mount Florida goal. Leap and downward header by Willie Waddell to Jimmy Delaney who bundled it through from five yards.

Opposite
This is how it happened - superb full-back turned author, Danny McGrain looks at the record in a bookseller's window

Of course not all the Celtic internationalists have been Scots. Quite a few were produced by Celtic for Ireland and indeed the 1950s was a vintage period for this with Bertie Peacock and Charlie Tully figuring prominently at Windsor Park. Before that of course there had been the famous Willie Cook and Patsy Gallagher and even a Celtic reserve goalkeeper, Collins, got his call to the colours in 1921-22.

As football has become more cosmopolitan, Danish and Icelandic internationals have taken the field for Celtic and the way the game is going, this may widen to take in other countries. There have of course also been the two Poles, the two Dariuses, Dziekanowski and Wdowyczk.

And what of individual contributions to matches? I remember Bobby Evans getting on top of the great Peter Doherty in a match against Ireland at Hampden in 1948-49 and almost single-handedly driving the Scots on to a 3-2 win which eventually brought us the Triple Crown. I remember John McPhail playing magnificently in a match against Wales, a model example of leading a line but his play was too intelligent for the Committee of the day, and the more robust Billy Houliston of Queen of the South was preferred.

Frank Haffey had a dreadful Wembley in 1961 but his defence was of singularly little help and in any event his own jittery nervy display against England the year before should have been evidence that he was being asked to take on a role for which in the last analysis he was under-equipped.

I remember the twisting Peter Shilton save which kept out a rocket from a Scot which would have given us a last-minute draw. The Scot? Danny McGrain – not the first name that would come

Opposite
Every inch a captain – the young Billy McNeill leads his team out at Parkhead followed by goalkeeper Frank Haffey and full-back Jim Kennedy

to mind for ferocity of shooting. Readers used to ask me when we would learn to use Kenny Dalglish properly (about six years was the answer) but he was to become one of the few players who would have been selected for the national side in the leading European countries.

Most people would have said that Roy Aitken was much less gifted than Dalglish as a player and yet this man of tremendous spirit, whose selection had been bitterly opposed, ended up probably the best Scot at the World Cup in Italy in 1990. It was a refreshing demonstration of the fact that while a basic competence must be there, other factors are needed.

There is disappointment that two of the most skilful players, namely Paul McStay and Charlie Nicholas, have not been able to leave that indelible stamp on international football that their extraordinary talents would have led one to believe. And to come right up to date will John Collins and Tom Boyd be able to take the ultimate step more easily?

As they say in the soaps, time will reveal all and in the coming season of 1994-95 the whole side will have abundant opportunity to get acquainted with the national stadium and perhaps share the fortunes of Pat Bonner who has contributed to the highs and lows of his country's cause at the very top level.

INTERNATIONALS AND INTERNATIONALISTS

HYNDLAND (Glasgow) Am I correct in saying that Bobby Hogg, when with Celtic was chosen as reserve in attendance for internationals more often than any player in Great Britain?. How often was he capped?

Bobby Hogg had only one full cap, against Czechoslovakia at Ibrox in 1937. He was also selected twice against the Football League and three times against the Irish League. He was chosen as reserve many times but I regret not having taken a complete tally to enable me to give a clear-cut answer. Dougie Gray of Rangers must have come quite near him for reserve selections.

STRATHIE BAR (Bridgeton) Did Jimmy Delaney score in an international against European opposition before 1939?

He had both Scottish goals in a 2-0 defeat of Germany at Ibrox in October 1936.

GENERAL WOLFE (Glasgow) Have Celtic ever provided six members of a Scottish League side against the Football League? If so were there any Rangers players in that same team?

Against the Football League in March 1920 Shaw, McNair, Dodds, Cringan, McMenemy and McAtee were all in the side as were Gordon and Cunningham of Rangers which did not prevent the Football League winning 4-0.

REGAL BAR (Clydebank) Can you name the first Celtic player to score for Scotland against England at Wembley?

When Bobby Lennox got one of Scotland's three goals against England in a 3-2 win in 1967 he was the first Celtic player to score in an international for Scotland at Wembley.

J. KEATING (Los Angeles) Did Charlie Tully ever play for Ireland when Frank Swift was in goal for England? I think the match was a 2-2 draw and Tully scored directly from a corner.

I can only trace them in opposition in the 1948 international which England won 6-2 in Belfast. Tully did not score, both the Irish goals going to Walsh of West Bromwich Albion.

NO.1. WESTERN ISLES (Oban) How many times did Patsy

Always the bridesmaid – Bobby Hogg, a fine right-back of the 1930s whose fate was to be an almost permanent travelling reserve for Scottish international teams

Gallagher appear in a blue jersey for Rangers or Scotland?

I have no record of appearances for Rangers as presumably these would be in friendly matches. He could not play for Scotland as he was ineligible, having been born in Ireland, but he appeared twice for the Scottish League against the Irish League and made several appearances for the unofficial Scottish side which visited Canada and the United States in 1927.

WEE VICS (Stevenston) When did Billy McNeill get his last cap as a full Scottish international and who was Scottish manager at the time? I say he was never selected by Tommy Docherty.

Wrong. McNeill's last three international caps, in the Home International series of 1972 were obtained when Tommy Docherty was in charge of the Scottish team.

DELANEY'S DONKEY (Renfrew) In Jock Stein's time did Celtic ever have six players in a full international side? If so please give the Scotland team.

There were six Celtic players in this side which beat Northern Ireland 2-1 at Hampden on November 16, 1967, Ferguson (Kilmarnock), Greig, (Rangers), Gemmell, Murdoch (both Celtic), McKinnon (Rangers), Clark (Celtic), Henderson (Rangers), Bremner (Leeds United), Chalmers, McBride, Lennox (all Celtic). Scorers for Scotland were Murdoch and Lennox.

VICTORIA BAR (Glasgow) How many positions did Willie Fernie play in in the Scottish international side? My mate says he only turned out as a forward.

Fernie was capped in no fewer than five positions, both wing-half positions, inside-right, inside-left and outside-left in an international career spanning the seasons 1953-54 to 1957-58.

PLUM (Mossend) Did Jimmy Quinn play for Scotland in any other position except centre-forward?

In 1908 he played against England at Hampden at outside-left.

ARTHUR McKELL (Craigend) I say that Charlie Tully played at outside-right in a winning Irish team at Wembley. Am I right?

Afraid not. Tully's only appearance at Wembley was in 1955 when he was inside-left in an Irish side which lost 3-0.

CLEEVES (Glasgow) How many caps did Bobby Murdoch get for Scotland and how many goals did he score?

Capped 12 times for Scotland, Bobby Murdoch found the net on five occasions.

B.B. (Glasgow) How many goals did Jimmy McGrory score in his career and how many times was he capped for Scotland?

In his career he scored 550 goals but incredibly was capped a meagre seven times, all against home international countries.

DRESSER (Dennistoun) I maintain that when Johnny Crum played against England at Wembley he was picked out of position in 1938.

He did not play in 1938 but two years before he was at outside-right in a 1-1 draw at a time when his normal position in the Celtic side was inside-left. Jimmy McGrory was still the normal Celtic centre-forward in 1936.

One of the greatest ever Celts – Jimmy Delaney shows off his Scottish, English and Irish Cup Winners medals and his finalists medal from the Republic of Ireland, a unique collection

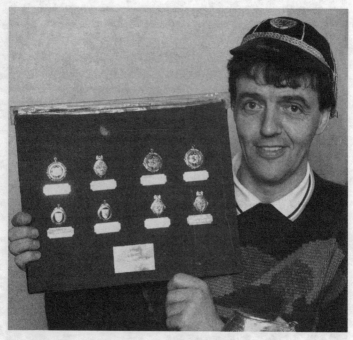

Frank McGarvey, brave and unselfish, displays his caps and medals

CHAPTER FIFTEEN

Great Players and Servants

What is star quality? Easy to recognise, difficult to define. It is what sets certain people apart so that their place in history is often curiously distorted. The Celtic support have had their favourites since Day One – names such as Sandy McMahon and Dan Doyle come readily to mind. But then the flamboyant player has always more chance of establishing himself in the record books.

Jimmy Quinn was a quiet, strong man who let his playing performances do the talking. The miner from Croy, or as Maley using the older word once decribed him, the collier, was a physically hard but very fair player to whom his sending off against Rangers was seen as a real stain on his character as a professional footballer.

One imagines that Patsy Gallagher would have borne such a dismissal more light-heartedly. Certainly he did not regard his war work in World War One too seriously, being fined and suspended from football for failure to turn up at his munition factory and throughout his career he tended to the skilful and the mischievous. For the former quality it is enough to cite the marvellous winning goal in the 1925 Cup Final against Dundee which in ice hockey terms he scored unassisted, and for the mischief on the occasion, like something out of *Charley's Aunt*, when he broke out of training disguised as an old lady.

To win acceptance players usually have to spend some considerable time with a club. Jimmy McMenemy certainly did

that and having acquired six Scottish Cup medals with Celtic he went on to become the only man to win a playing medal in the Cup while basically a trainer, which was primarily his function when he moved on to Partick Thistle.

The "jersey player" was a more common phenomon then and this partly explains why Jimmy McGrory is held in such high esteem. Above all else he was a Celt. He was also a thoroughly good man in a sphere of activity where goodness and ability are by no means always inseparable. I still wait to hear anyone in football make an adverse comment about Jimmy McGrory. So true was this that the support seemed quite happy with his managership although in no real sense did he exercise control.

Of the fine 1938 side perhaps Jimmy Delaney was the most enduringly popular and it was an ominous sign when at the very beginning of peacetime football in 1946 he opted to go to Manchester United. The wartime period was so generally depressing that only one real hero emerges from it – the frighteningly brave and athletic Willie Miller who so often prevented bad from becoming embarrassing. Malcolm MacDonald, always well thought of at Parkhead during this time, demonstrated that at least one other player remembered what acceptable pre-war standards were.

Back in the days of peace Tully mania descended. Looked at dispassionately his actual achievements were not all that many. Balding, rarely fit in the modern sense, and most certainly not fast, Charlie Tully nevertheless became the subject of idolatry. Why? Because he was skilful, because he absolutely believed himself to be better than his opponent of the moment and because he gave back to the team the most priceless of footballing qualities,

Opposite
The greatest of them all? Sir Robert Kelly certainly thought that of Patsy Gallagher, seen here against Airdrie, and many of Sir Robert's generation would have been in full accord

John Hughes is serious, Jim Craig and Willie Wallace more relaxed as the bus is boarded for an away match

Opposite
The wee barra! Bobby Collins, living proof that if you're good enough, you're big enough

confidence. He was backed by Bobby Collins, the pocket Atlas, (only Dalglish has been as skilful and durable in the front line) and the great-hearted Bobby Evans who very possibly pounded more turf than any other player in the club's history.

The Lisbon Lions of course go into the Hall of Fame *en masse* but the crowd's attitude was interesting to some of the fringe players of that time. Charlie Gallagher was a highly intelligent player whereas John Hughes was marvellously instinctive. But the terracings were more forgiving of errors by Yogi than they were of Charlie's. Later two very fine players indeed, Harry Hood and Tom Callaghan, who were taking Celtic into modern methods were sometimes roughly treated by the Jungle and surrounding districts.

Billy McNeill, probably the best-ever Celtic captain, retired on a high after a Cup Final while the human dynamo, Bobby Lennox played on and performed at top level until he could almost have been playing with the sons of the men who had been his team-mates in 1967.

Every so often a player comes along who is recognised as exceptional by even the most grudging of his team-mates. Such was Kenny Dalglish who from the word go seemed incapable of being overawed by any situation or any opposition. There are a few players who are untransferrable in the sense that the support will never be reconciled to or forgive their going and in Dalglish's case this was certainly so. It may very well be that eventually in Desmond White's phrase, "there was no way of keeping Kenny Dalglish at Parkhead" but his going caused a loss of confidence which at best has only been partially regained.

The McAvennies, the McGarveys, the MacLeods, all have their backers. And the player whose honesty shines out for all to see, the Roy Aitkens and the Sean Fallons of an earlier age, will not lack for support. Those who have spent a lifetime at the club deserve regard. There will be relief in this summer of 1994 that Paddy Bonner is staying on and it is hard to imagine Paul McStay in other colours.

There are two other categories of player who stay in the

memory more than might be reckoned. The first falls into the category of "if only we had got him sooner" and contains such names as Ronnie Simpson, Pat Stanton and Billy Stark. The other group is of those whose careers were curtailed, by death in the cases of John Thomson, Peter Scarff, John Millsop and Johnny Doyle, by injury in the cases of John Higgins, Billy McPhail and, even in their late 30s, Ronnie Simpson and Jock Stein.

This is a category, Great Players, where things may well change over the next few years as it becomes less and less fashionable for players to see out their careers with the one club. Fans need time to get to know players and it is difficult to establish a rapport with players who are in and out of a revolving door. Perhaps clubs might care to reflect that while too much stability in playing personnel can cause complacency, too little can cause a confusion and failure to achieve.

It is also true of course that another kind of player figures in the letters and that is what might be described as the spectacularly bad buy. I had thought of suggesting such an eleven drawn from the last ten years, but decided you would do a better job, so in the words of W S Gilbert, "the task of filling up the blanks I'd rather leave to you!"

GREAT PLAYERS AND SERVANTS

KNOXY AND JERRY (Maryhill) My brother holds that Billy McNeill's first league goal for Celtic was scored against Dundee at Parkhead on March 3, 1962. I say it was against Ayr United at Somerset Park on March 4, 1961 when Celtic won 3-1.

You are correct and the Celtic scorers that day were McNeill in 55 minutes, Peacock (pen.) in 74 minutes and Fernie in 82 minutes.

VENDOR (Glasgow) Can you name the former Celtic players whose sons have followed them to Parkhead up until now (1969)?

There are only four, so far as I can recall, namely Jimmy McMenemy, Patsy Gallagher, Johnny Paton and Johnny Divers.

JIM FROM HAMILTON How long was Bobby Hogg with Celtic after leaving the junior club Royal Albert?

He was at Parkhead from 1931-48 when he moved on to Alloa.

TAM (Cumbernauld) Can you give Steve Chalmers date of birth and when he joined Celtic?

He became a senior at a comparatively late stage having been born on December 26, 1936 and joining Celtic from Ashfield in February 1959.

BIG TREE BAR (Coatbridge) I say that John Donnelly left Celtic after Neil Mochan had been transferred. Did Mochan play for Celtic when John Hughes had his first team debut?

Neil Mochan was transferred to Dundee United in November 1960 and John Donnelly to Preston North End in April 1962. The Celtic forward line against Third Lanark when John Hughes made his debut on August 13, 1960 read, Carroll, Chalmers, Hughes, Mochan, Divers.

BEE BEE (Glasgow) Has Steve Chalmers ever scored three goals against Rangers?

He did this in a 5-1 league victory at Parkhead on January 3, 1966. Gallagher and Murdoch had the other Celtic goals and Davie Wilson scored for Rangers.

TONY X (Falkirk) When was Pat Crerand transferred from Celtic to Manchester United?

Pat Crerand was signed by Manchester United on February 6, 1963 and the transfer fee was given as £56,000.

FITZY (Govan) For which clubs did Neil Mochan, the present Celtic coach (1972) play?

His clubs in order were Morton, Middlesbrough, Celtic, Dundee United and Raith Rovers.

Opposite
Paul Elliot was probably the best of the English signings made in the late 1980s but he left the club on less than amicable terms

ANDY (Glasgow) When did the great Jimmy Quinn retire from the game? I say he stopped playing in 1913.

Willie Maley in "The Story of Celtic" says that Quinn retired during the 1914-15 season after 14 years service at Parkhead.

OLD TIMER (Thornliebank) Can you tell me which junior club Patsy Gallagher played with and when he left the junior ranks?

He was with his local club, Clydebank Juniors and he finished playing with them in November 1911.

O.A.P. (Clydebank) Can you give the date of Patsy Gallagher's last game for Celtic before going to Falkirk?

His last appearance in the green and white hoops was against Clyde at Parkhead on October 10, 1925.

RAY (Helensburgh) If Bertie Auld played for Dumbarton after he had signed for Celtic can you give the number of league games he played for the Boghead club?

Bertie Auld was lent by Celtic to Dumbarton in October 1956 and before he returned to Parkhead at the end of the season he had played in 15 league matches and one Scottish Cup tie.

G. McAFFREY (Alexandria) Please give details of Willie Wallace's career with Raith Rovers, Hearts and Celtic.

For Raith Rovers he made 58 league appearances and scored 23 goals. With Hearts he scored 119 goals in all matches and made 171 league appearances. For Celtic he played 134 league games plus six substitutions and in them he scored 88 goals.

HUGHIE (Glasgow) When did Bobby Lennox first appear in Celtic's first team?

I make his first competitive appearance to have been in a league match against Dundee at Parkhead on March 3, 1962 when he scored one of the goals in a 2-1 win against the eventual league winners.

BIG ALFIE (Gorbals) When did Kenny Dalglish sign for Liverpool and what was the transfer fee?

£440,000 changed hands when Kenny Dalglish went south in August 1977.

GENTLEMAN JIMMY (Linwood) When and where did Jimmy McGrory play his first match for Celtic?

His debut was against Third Lanark at Cathkin on January 21, 1923.

PETER KEARNEY (Glasgow) When did Patsy Gallagher and Jimmy Delaney leave Celtic for Falkirk?

Patsy Gallagher went to Brockville in the course of season 1926-27. Jimmy Delaney became a Bairn in 1953 but before that he had been with Manchester United and Aberdeen.

OLD ROWLEY (Renfrew) Did Kenny Dalglish win the English Football Writers and English Professional Footballers Association Player of the Year Awards in the same year?

He brought off this double in 1983 having previously won the Writers Award in 1979.

SWITCH HITTER (Muirend) Did Harry Hood as a Celtic player ever score a hat-trick against Rangers?

He had all three goals in the 3-1 League Cup semi-final win against Rangers at Hampden on December 5, 1973.

W.P.C. (Govan) When did Danny McGrain of Celtic fracture his skull and what was the opposing team involved?

Danny McGrain suffered a serious head injury at Brockville on March 25, 1972 in a league match which Celtic won 1-0, Vic Davidson getting the winner.

ALSO WROTE (Coatbridge) Did Bertie Auld and Sean Fallon ever play in the same team?

Yes, on several occasions in season 1957-58. Two games that spring to mind are a 1-0 win at Brockville on September 7 and a 1-1 draw against Aberdeen on January 18 at Parkhead.

ADAMSLIE (Kirkintilloch) When did Bobby Evans make his first-team debut for Celtic? Was he an inside-forward for several years before moving to right-half?

He first appeared against Albion Rovers in a Southern League game in August 1944 at Cliftonhill. For about his first three seasons at Parkhead he was normally at inside-forward.

KING KENNY (Glasgow) I read that until now (March 1985) Kenny Dalglish has played 750 games for Liverpool. How many did he play for Celtic?

I only have the figures for league matches and of these he played

202 plus 2 substitutions. If you said he had about 300 first-team appearances altogether for Celtic you would not be far out. I have just got all his Celtic figures to hand and in addition to the 204 league games he played 31 Scottish Cup, 60 League Cup and 29 European matches, 324 in all which produced 167 goals for the club.

Copies of pictures in this book are available from:

Photo Sales Dept.
Evening Times
195 Albion Street
Glasgow G1 1QP